STEVEN SPIELBERG

Filmmaker

FERGUSON
CAREER BIOGRAPHIES

STEVEN SPIELBERG

Filmmaker

James Robert Parish

Ferguson
An imprint of Facts On File

Steven Spielberg: Filmmaker

Ferguson
An imprint of Facts On File, Inc.
132 West 31st Street
New York NY 10001

Parish, James Robert.
Steven Spielberg, filmmaker / James Robert Parish.
p. cm. — (Ferguson career biographies)
Includes index.
Summary: A biography of Steven Spielberg, the Academy Award-winning producer and director of films in a variety of genres, such as E.T., Jaws, Saving Private Ryan, and Schindler's List.
ISBN 0-8160-5481-9 (hc: alk. paper)
1. Spielberg, Steven, 1946— Juvenile literature. 2. Motion picture producers and directors—United States—Biography—Juvenile literature. [1. Spielberg, Steven, 1946– 2. Producers and directors.] I. Title. II. Series.
PN1998.3.S65P37 2004
791.43'0233'092--dc22 2003015338

Ferguson books are available at special discounts when purchased in bulk quantities for businesses, associations, institutions, or sales promotions. Please call our Special Sales Department in New York at (212) 967-8800 or (800) 322-8755.

You can find Ferguson on the World Wide Web at http://www.fergpubco.com

Text design by David Strelecky

Pages 119–147 adapted from Ferguson's *Encyclopedia of Careers and Vocational Guidance, Twelfth Edition*

Printed in the United States of America

MP FOF 10 9 8 7 6 5 4 3 2 1

This book is printed on acid-free paper.

CONTENTS

1

A SUPREME FILMMAKER

In mid-2003 for its annual ranking of "The 100 Most Powerful People in Movies" *Premiere* magazine placed filmmaker Steven Spielberg at the top of its list. In making this rating, the magazine described Spielberg as a "culture-shaping, blockbuster-making, Oscar-winning, studio-owning icon of cinema." To date, Spielberg's feature films have grossed over $3.1 billion at the domestic box office, making him the most commercially successful moviemaker in the history of American cinema.

Knowing the Audience

Spielberg, who has won two Best Director Academy Awards to date, is a talented craftsman whose artistic vision has shaped and been shaped by the sensibilities of the average filmgoer. Spielberg has a great ability to play upon people's hopes, fears, and shared experiences in a compelling way. Over the decades he has worked in many movie genres, including thriller (*Jaws*, 1975), science fiction (*Close Encounters of the Third Kind,* 1977), farce (*1941*, 1979), adventure (*Raiders of the Lost Ark,* 1981), horror (*Poltergeist*, 1982), drama (*Schindler's List*, 1993), war (*Saving Private Ryan*, 1998), and action (*Minority Report*, 2002). No matter what type of motion picture he undertakes, he instinctively looks for those underlying elements that can be best appreciated by most of the audience.

Searching to Improve Himself

Like most serious artists, Spielberg is always searching to improve his creative output. He admits that he is never fully satisfied with his past pictures, despite the fact they have pleased millions of viewers. According to Steven: "I can watch my own movies up to a point, and then I become too critical about choices and missed opportunities and better shots, that a year later seem more vivid in my mind than what I'd remembered a year before."

Spielberg has been consistently successful from early in his career. However, he has come to accept that his many achievements in the entertainment industry at a relatively young age may have distracted him from greater artistic goals over the years. In accepting the honorary Irving G. Thalberg Academy Award in March 1987 for "creative producing," he observed, "Most of my life has

Steven Spielberg accepts the Irving G. Thalberg Academy Award. (Photofest)

been spent in the dark watching movies. Movies have been the literature of my life." While in his forties, he realized the following about himself and his generation: "In our romance with technology and our excitement at exploring all the possibilities of film and video, I think we've partially lost something that we now have to reclaim. I think it's time to renew our romance with the word. I'm as culpable as anyone of exalting the image at the expense of the word." In other words, Steven wanted to make the emotions—the artistic center—in his films just as compelling as the visual elements for which he became famous. Receiving the prestigious Oscar tribute, he said, "reminds me of how much growth as an artist I have ahead of me in order to be worthy of standing in the company of those who have received this before me." He realized that, as a primary maker of mass entertainment, he has a responsibility to stimulate moviegoers' intellect as well as amusing them. This strong moral obligation has since become a key factor in all of Spielberg's endeavors: as filmmaker, studio owner, business entrepreneur, charity giver, and family man.

2

MOVIES AS A WAY OF LIFE

Steven Allan Spielberg was born December 18, 1946, in Cincinnati, Ohio. He was the first-born child of Arnold and Leah (Posner) Spielberg, followed by three sisters: Anne (1949), Sue (1953), and Nancy (1956). Steven's first three years were spent in Avondale, a suburb of Cincinnati with a large Jewish community.

Family Influences

From his earliest years, Steven's family life formed enduring memories, wishes, and frustrations, many of which would find their way eventually into the screen works of this future filmmaker. Steven's father, an electrical engineer, and his mother, a former concert pianist, were emotional opposites. Their contrasting approaches to life had a great effect on their son. Steven's dad was a workaholic, constantly concerned with providing for his family.

Arnold Spielberg was usually too preoccupied with his career in technology to focus much attention on his gifted boy who, from an early age, was always asking questions, wanting to know about everything.

In contrast, Leah Spielberg, with her strong love of the creative arts, was a doting and somewhat eccentric mother who overindulged her youngest child. Steven learned quickly how to win his way with her and others in the household. It set a pattern for life. Years later Leah said, "I didn't know that everybody didn't have kids like him. . . . If I had known better, I would have taken him to a psychiatrist, and there never would have been an *E.T.*"

Philip and Jennie Posner, Steven's maternal grandparents, also pampered him. His grandfather was an able storyteller who entranced his grandson with accounts of his immigration from Russia to America decades earlier, and explanations of the family's Orthodox Jewish roots in the old country. (These colorful stories later inspired Spielberg's animated feature, *An American Tail* [1986].) Philip's gift for spinning tales was passed on to his grandson.

Grandmother Jennie, who loved going to the movies, taught English to survivors of the Holocaust—the victims of Nazi persecution during World War II. Often, while visiting his grandparents' home, Steven heard from these adult "students" firsthand narratives of the brutality they had suffered in Europe during the 1930s and 1940s. These vivid descriptions made a deep impression on the boy and later helped to shape his interest in making *Schindler's List* as a motion picture.

Imagination and Change

When Steven was three years old, the family moved to Camden, New Jersey, where Mr. Spielberg had accepted a position with the RCA Corporation. This was the first of several emotionally jarring changes in young Steven's life. As he has recalled, "Just as I'd become accustomed to a school and a teacher and a best friend, the For Sale sign would dig into the front lawn. . . . And it would always be that inevitable good-bye scene." (Spielberg would also say, "The older I got the harder it got.") By the age of four, the insecure youngster had become a nail-biter, a habit that he still has.

Possessing a tremendous imagination, the boy was spooked by his new environment. "I was afraid of trees, clouds, the wind, the dark." In particular, there was a raggedy maple tree outside his bedroom window, which at nighttime—due to the nearby streetlights—created creepy shadows on the walls of his room. Steven found the tree to be menacing. He also was convinced that sinister ghosts lurked under his bed, in the closet, and in a large crack on the wall. Even such a harmless toy as a clown doll took on frightening overtones in his vivid imagination. These intense feelings of being scared led to some of the frightening scenes in Spielberg's film *Poltergeist*.

Steven saw his first movie in 1952, the year the Spielbergs moved to a house in Haddon Township, a few miles from Camden. His father took him to see *The Greatest Show on Earth,* a film about circus performers. At first the youngster was disappointed to discover that the real-life circus he thought he was going to witness was actually just flickering images on a screen. However, he quickly became fascinated by the movie spectacle, especially by a scene showing a gigantic train wreck. Steven, with his active imagination, was awed and frightened by what he had seen in the film, just as he would be by films such as Walt Disney's *Bambi* and *Snow White and the Seven Dwarfs*.

What amazed Steven the most about movies was how a plot unfolding on the big screen could absorb him completely. Later, when Spielberg became a filmmaker, one of his goals would be to make audiences feel "transported" by the picture, just as he had been so effectively transported as a child.

Finding Entertainment

When not reading comic books, practicing magic tricks in the basement, building model planes, joining neighborhood friends in playing war games with toy soldiers, or deliberately frightening his young sisters with eerie stories, Steven was a devout TV watcher. His father tried to persuade him to spend more time studying—especially mathematics, which Steven dreaded—but the boy was preoccupied with watching television.

Sometimes, to bond with his son and draw him away from the television, Mr. Spielberg would describe his own adventures during World War II. The elder Spielberg had been a serviceman in the Southeast Asian country of Burma fighting the Japanese, who were then the enemy. His father's vivid accounts had a great impact on Steven's future work and artistic sensibilities. Regarding World War II and the 1940s in general, Steven has said, "I love that period. . . . It was the end of an era, the end of innocence, and I have been clinging to it for most of my adult life."

In early 1957 the Spielbergs moved yet again because of the father's career. This time they relocated across the country to Phoenix, Arizona. They soon took up residence in a ranch-style house that would be the inspiration for the homes shown in several of the budding moviemaker's works: *Close Encounters of the Third Kind*, *Poltergeist*, and *E.T. the Extra-Terrestrial* (1982). If Steven had felt displaced before, when his family had moved from Ohio to New Jersey, he felt more so now in this conservative Arizona community where there were few other Jewish families. At school, because he considered himself a nerd and was not good at sports, he felt different and left out. As a result, he withdrew more into himself.

However, one of the most astonishing adventures of Steven's childhood occurred not long after the Spielbergs relocated to the Grand Canyon state. Late one evening, his dad woke him up and told him to get dressed. Without further explanation, the two drove off in Mr. Spielberg's car. A half-hour later they pulled over to the side of the road. Spreading a blanket on the ground, they lay down and looked up at the night sky. Steven's father pointed at a wondrous meteor shower that was in progress. While his dad gave Steven a technical explanation for the spellbinding occurrence, the boy was entranced by the sight of these magical "falling stars." Years later, this heavenly display would be the inspiration for the spectacular images in Spielberg's feature film *Close Encounters of the Third Kind*.

Not long after settling into their residence in Arcadia, a section of Phoenix, Steven became absorbed with the eight-millimeter movie camera that his dad had received recently as a gift from Mrs. Spielberg. (It was a simple, fixed-focus model, typical of this time before the invention of video camcorders, digital cameras, and the like.) Intrigued with his new hobby, the youngster began filming diaries of the family's weekend camping trips.

Soon Steven was making short movies for his own amusement and, in the process, learning more about this

The Arizona night sky of Spielberg's childhood inspired scenes such as this one, from Close Encounters of the Third Kind. (Photofest)

exciting craft. One of his first personal efforts was the three-minute *The Last Train Wreck*, which showed his electric trains crashing into one another. Even at this early age, he had a natural instinct for the camera. He would edit his "stories" in the camera, stopping the filming to set up the next sequence in his little story. Another of the youngster's early films was based on asking his indulgent mother to boil several cans of cherry pie filling in her kitchen pressure cooker. When the ingredients eventually exploded, Steven gleefully captured the red, juicy mess on camera. This was a sneak preview of an interest in special effects that would become an important part of Steven's directorial style. (He left it to his lenient mother to clean up the cherry goo all over the kitchen.)

The Amateur Filmmaker

While Spielberg was not the only youth in his neighborhood making home movies, he was certainly among the most persistent. In 1958, he was a member of the local Boy Scout troop. To win a merit badge in photography, he made his own western (*The Last Gunfight*). A major prop in this nine-minute silent entry was a red stagecoach stationed outside a steakhouse restaurant in nearby Scottsdale. Not only did Steven convince his dad to help organize the film venture, but he also persuaded neighborhood youngsters to appear in the story.

What especially impressed Steven about this movie shoot was that, by being in charge of the little film, he could command the attention of other children who often ignored him in daily life. Even more exciting for Spielberg, was his discovery that through the filmmaking process he could make "something happen that I could relive over and over again, something that would only be a memory without a camera in my hand." When the finished result (which had cost $8.50) was screened for the Boy Scouts, the audience was enthusiastic. Steven was thrilled! It made him more obsessed than ever with filmmaking.

To earn money to pay for the raw materials for his picture-making activity, 12-year-old Steven showed rented professional movies to the neighborhood kids. His parents and sisters helped with the home theater, even making and selling refreshments. While Mr. Spielberg insisted that the proceeds from the ticket sales be donated to charity, he allowed Steven to keep the profits from the refreshments.

In this period, Steven's most ambitious motion picture project was *Fighter Squad*, a World War II tale. Shot in black-and-white with a more advanced camera that his

World War II and the 1940s have always been some of Spielberg's favorite stories and film subjects. (U. S. National Archives)

dad had bought him, the 15-minute entry used stock footage from commercial documentaries of World War II dogfights. The sequences shot by the young filmmaker included scenes filmed at a local airport, where Mr. Spielberg had gained permission for Steven and his film crew to use a stationary vintage plane. In this short combat tale, scripter-director-cinematographer Steven appeared briefly as a German flier. The amateur film, which Steven had begun in the seventh grade, was completed by the following school year.

High School Troubles

By the time Steven had entered Arcadia High School in fall 1961, he was a determined filmmaker who had little interest in anything else (except perhaps reading science-fiction stories and watching TV). Now he was clashing more frequently with his dad who wanted him to follow in his technology career footsteps, but the teenager had little interest in chemistry or math. Because Steven did not belong to the popular crowd, he felt himself an outsider, even though there were many other students like him. One refuge for Spielberg was the school's drama group where he did not have to fit into molds that he thought were unsuitable or impossible for him to attain. Even there, he rarely won acting assignments because he was too awkward performing onstage.

Sensitive about his gawky looks and his clumsiness at athletics, in high school Steven became strongly conscious of anti-Semitism and how this irrational dislike (or even hatred) of Jews further branded him as an "alien" among his fellow students. (By now, some of his schoolmates had taken to calling this uncommon individual "Spielbug.") Making matters worse, his parents were undergoing a stressful period in their marriage. Often, when Mr. Spielberg was home from his frequent business trips, the tension in the household was so strong that it could not be hidden from the children.

Because he didn't want to deal with this increasingly painful emotional situation at home over which he had no control, Steven escaped more into his moviemaking, which gave his life hope and meaning. Because his parents were caught up in their own problems, they gave their son, in particular, more freedom than most youths his age would have had. He used the relaxed supervision to focus on his moviemaking—sometimes at the expense of his schoolwork. While he wasn't the best student, the young Spielberg's creativity and dedication to filmmaking gave him a sense of accomplishment and confidence during this troubling time. Steven would comment in later years, "I was surrounded by so much negativity when I was a kid that I had no recourse but to be positive."

Escape to Nowhere

In 1959, Steven had begun shooting an ambitious World War II film in color. *Escape to Nowhere* was finally completed three years later. Much of the 40-minute entry was shot in the desert near Camelback Mountain (outside of Phoenix) as well as at a nearby Western studio when it was not in use. Set in 1940s' North Africa, the picture focuses on a squad of American soldiers outnumbered by their German enemies. Steven again persuaded classmates to appear in his picture. His household was also an important part of the movie venture: the parents took turns driving the family jeep while wearing Nazi costumes. Even his sister Anne had a brief role as a German infantryman.

For Steven, an exciting part of this film was the use of explosions for the battle scenes. The budding cinema director would enthuse later, "My special effects were great!" Even more impressive was the fact that he persuaded the class bully to play the role of the squadron leader. During filming, at least, the tables were turned: Steven's frequent tormentor was under the demanding control of "Spielbug."

Escape to Nowhere was entered in a statewide amateur film competition and it won first prize. The award included a 16-millimeter camera that Steven exchanged for a more economical, but highly equipped, Bolex-H8 eight-millimeter model. His dad paid for a sound system to go along with the new gear. Now Steven could record sound directly onto film.

A "Major" Production

From mid-to-late 1962, the high school student used his new equipment to film *Firelight*. Based on his own 67-page screenplay, the science-fiction story was reminiscent of the many sci-fi pictures he had watched in the 1950s. Often filming at nighttime to avoid the summer heat and then on weekends during the school year, Steven relied on fellow students from the school drama club to flesh out the roles he'd written. The narrative concerns a scientist and his wife engulfed in domestic problems, a fanatical UFO expert, as well as individuals abducted by aliens who use a powerful firelight. (Much of this story premise would find its way into Spielberg's "remake" of the picture: *Close Encounters of the Third Kind.*)

Steven found great satisfaction in solving the film's many technical problems. In particular, he rose to the challenge of creating the special effects for the movie's mysterious energy forces used to either abduct or destroy earthlings. Once the shoot was completed, Steven—with the advice of his father and his father's business associates from General Electric—added sound effects, music, and dialogue to his production.

The Spielbergs supported their son's impressive creative venture by renting the Phoenix Little Theatre to premiere the boy's feature film. On the evening of March 24, 1964, the two-hour-and-15-minute *Firelight* was shown to an enthusiastic audience who each paid 75 cents admission (which put the under $600 production into a slight profit). Local newspapers appreciatively reviewed the movie. Flush with success, Steven was convinced of what he desired as his life career. "I wanted Hollywood," he said.

However, first Steven had to deal with the latest change in the routine of his life. The day after the *Firelight* showing, the family moved again, this time to northern California. His parents, in a last-ditch effort to save their faltering marriage, relocated the household to Los Gatos so Mr. Spielberg could accept a position with IBM at its San Jose plant. Steven completed his academic year at the local California high school. That summer the family changed addresses yet again, this time into a more upscale home in nearby affluent Saratoga.

The Studio Lot and Helpful Friends

Hollywood legend has it that Steven Spielberg broke into the entertainment business by sneaking onto the Universal Studios film lot in 1969. Once on the studio grounds, he supposedly located an empty bungalow office and set up temporary headquarters. Then, through various ruses, he sneaked onto the facility on a daily basis for two years, establishing himself with various casts and crews on the lot. Another legend says that while visiting the Universal Studios Tour in the summer of 1965, Steven ambled away from the tram ride and browsed around the lot. While wandering onto a soundstage, he supposedly encountered Charles A. "Chuck" Silvers of the studio's editorial department, and it was Silvers who arranged a pass for Spielberg to return the next day to show him a few of his home movies.

In actuality, it was through an acquaintance of his father that Steven was introduced to Chuck Silvers sometime between the fall of 1963 and spring 1964. Silvers was intrigued by this energetic young man who had written, directed, and photographed his own movies. When Steven returned to Arizona, he and Silvers occasionally corresponded. After *Firelight* was completed, Spielberg returned to Universal to show the film to Silvers, who was extremely impressed, especially by the young man's use of stop-motion animation. (This was a difficult process in which miniature figures were moved a fraction of an inch at a time, with each new position being filmed for one or more frames. By combining these shots the desired motion effect was created when the footage was played back at normal speed.)

As Silvers has recalled of Spielberg, "There was no doubt that he was special. There was this tremendous confidence everything was going to work out the way he wanted it."

During the summer of 1964, thanks to contacts made through his new mentor, Steven worked as an unpaid clerical assistant in the Universal editorial department. This job enabled him to wander around the vast studio lot where he watched feature films and TV shows being shot. Whenever possible, he chatted with technicians. These craftspeople—including editors and postproduction personnel—were often so impressed by this eager newcomer that they made a special effort to explain various aspects of the filmmaking

The Universal Studios lot in the 1960s. (Photofest)

profession. This experience gave the enthusiastic student a private tutorial in the profession he intended to join. He also made many contacts who could help him borrow the photography equipment he needed, as well as provide ways to develop his amateur movies at the studio's film labs. Nevertheless, Spielberg was frustrated that he could not persuade studio executives or experienced filmmakers to talk with him or to look at his motion pictures.

A Year of Horror

Consumed by his growing ambitions of becoming a filmmaker, Steven had little interest in academics at Saratoga High School. Also, he was heavily distracted by personal problems. Besides coping with the effects of his parents' unhappy marriage, he once again felt himself to be the isolated stranger in the classroom and in his new neighborhood in California. Although he refused to discuss the situation for years to come, he was victimized by several intolerant classmates. They disliked him not only because he was nerdy, but also because he was Jewish. As a result, he was the victim of both verbal and physical abuse. The unpleasant situation strongly affected the newcomer whose greatest desire was to fit in with his non-Jewish peers. Rather than express his anger toward his detractors, he used a maneuver employed by countless other people over the centuries—humor. However, his smart-mouthed remarks usually just annoyed his tormentors and often made the situation worse.

Steven in high school. (Classmates.com/Yearbook Archives)

Besides the escape provided by his filmmaking activities, Steven found some relief from his problems at school when he served as a sports reporter on the school newspaper and participated in the backstage squad for a class play. The unhappy student graduated from high school in June 1965.

Moving on to College

Spielberg hoped to attend a prominent film school after graduating high school. However, his grades had been mediocre and both the University of California–Los Angeles and the University of Southern California rejected him. Because he knew that if he did not attend college he would be drafted into military service and likely serve in the escalating conflict in Vietnam, he applied to California State College at Long Beach. What attracted him to that southern California campus, which had no cinema program at the time, was its proximity to Universal Studios—about an hour's drive away.

About the time that Steven graduated from high school, his father left the household and accepted a new job in Los Angeles. Within the next year, Steven's parents divorced. As part of the divorce settlement, it was agreed that Arnold be given custody of Steven, while the three girls would remain with their mother. Mrs. Spielberg soon moved back to Phoenix and, in 1967, wed a longtime family friend, Bernie Adler.

During his freshman year of college Steven commuted between Brentwood (where his father had an apartment) and the Long Beach campus. When not attending classes, he hung around the sets at Universal as an unpaid worker. On those three days a week that he spent on the lot, he often slept overnight in a studio office. He kept a spare change of clothes with him so that he could look fresh in the morning as he made his unofficial rounds at the busy facility.

While father and son initially got along well as roommates, Mr. Spielberg soon became upset by his son's lack of interest in being a serious college student. He wanted Steven to get a solid education and establish himself in a career that would provide security and respect. The more his dad pushed him to become a real student, the more resistant Steven became. Increasingly, the young man turned to Chuck Silvers at Universal as a substitute to his own father. In 1967, Spielberg left his father's apartment to share a house in West Los Angeles with Ralph Burris, an older student he had met on campus.

A Breakthrough Project

At Long Beach, Steven showed some interest in his major, which was English, although he was still not fond of reading books. However, he displayed little enthusiasm for his radio and TV classes, which were the closest courses to filmmaking that the school then offered. Instead, his energy went into his time spent at Universal.

Chuck Silvers finally convinced his protégée that no one of importance at Universal or elsewhere would take him seriously as a filmmaker until he shot a movie in the 35-millimeter professional format. With the support of his roommate Burris, who had dropped out of law school to seek a career as a movie producer, Spielberg began a sports-themed short film (*Slipstream*) in the spring of 1967. In choosing his topic—daring bicycle riders—Spielberg had none of the lofty artistic goals of his generation of up-and-coming filmmakers. Rather, Steven's aim was, "I want everybody to enjoy my films."

Unfortunately, Steven and his backers (which included his father) ran out of funds and the project had to be dropped. Nevertheless, Spielberg learned from the misadventure and, within a year, he and producer Burris were making a new short film, *Amblin'*. Using a cast and crew of amateurs, including Steven's sister Anne, who worked as continuity supervisor and caterer, the picture was shot at southern California locations in the summer of 1968. It was a compacted picture of life on the road involving a would-be hippie who meets a female drifter in the Mojave Desert. The two fall in love as they make their way to the Pacific coast. As a cost-saving device, *Amblin'* was shot without dialogue, but did use sound effects.

Once this project was finished, Spielberg screened the 22-minute entry for his mentor. Silvers was so awed by what he had just seen that he contacted Sidney J. Sheinberg, the young vice president of production for Universal Television. After much persuasion, Sheinberg viewed the short film. He, in turn, was so astonished by "the maturity and the warmth that was in that short," that he contacted Spielberg to set up a meeting.

During their conference, the executive told Steven, "You should be a director." Spielberg fully agreed. Before Steven left the office, Sheinberg offered the confident young man a seven-year studio contract. When Spielberg mentioned that he was still a student, Sheinberg asked, "Kid, do you want to go to college or do you want to direct?"

3

MAKING A NAME IN HOLLYWOOD— AND THE WORLD

In June 1969 Steven Spielberg's *Amblin'* was entered in the Atlanta Film Festival. It was selected as best live-action short subject. There was hope that the much-praised entry would go on to win a prestigious Academy Award nomination. However, this was not to be the case. This disappointment set a pattern for years to come: Despite the huge commercial successes of many of Spielberg's films, the Academy of Motion Picture Arts and Sciences (which bestows the Academy Awards, or Oscars) often ignored his efforts.

A Tough Decision

Spielberg, who now had the services of a professional, major talent agency, needed to make a decision about his college status before he could actually begin his directing contract with Universal. Because he felt guilty at displeasing his parents (especially his father) by not completing his higher education, he suffered through the first semester of his junior year at Long Beach. However, by the end of January 1969, he left the campus for good in order to start work at Universal at a $275 weekly salary.

Even though he pursued this opportunity, Spielberg never forgot the importance of an education. Thirty-three years later, in May 2002, after a year of supervised independent study, he completed his course work at Long Beach and received a degree in Film and Electronic Media. In achieving this belated educational goal, Steven said, "I wanted to accomplish this for many years as a 'thank you' to my parents for giving me the opportunity for an education and a career."

At Work on the Soundstage

In the late 1960s Hollywood was changing from the old studio-run system of the 1930s and 1940s into the "new" Hollywood of corporations and independent filmmakers. In this transitional period it was still unusual for major studios to utilize young (often unproven) talent to direct screen fare—whether it be feature films or television product. However, the strong impression that Steven's *Amblin'* had made, plus the continued sponsorship of his new mentor, Universal executive Sidney Sheinberg, made all the difference in Spielberg's case. Steven became a person who could not be easily ignored.

For his professional debut Steven was assigned to direct one of the three parts of *Night Gallery*, a two-hour TV movie. Entitled "Eyes," his segment deals with a wealthy New York City woman who will do anything to regain her lost eyesight—even for just a short period of time. She undergoes a successful operation, but the irony is that when her bandages are removed, the city is suddenly blanketed in a blackout. This multipart, made-for-television feature was to be a pilot for a new TV series based on Rod Serling's classic 1950s program of the same name.

What made Steven's directing task so challenging was that the star of his *Night Gallery* segment was Joan Crawford. At age 64, the Oscar-winning star was a Hollywood legend and was known to be demanding and difficult. More than 40 years her junior, Steven worried that he was too inexperienced and would be at the mercy of this veteran celebrity. However, by studying up on her career and letting Crawford take charge of their first meeting, he won her cooperation on the project.

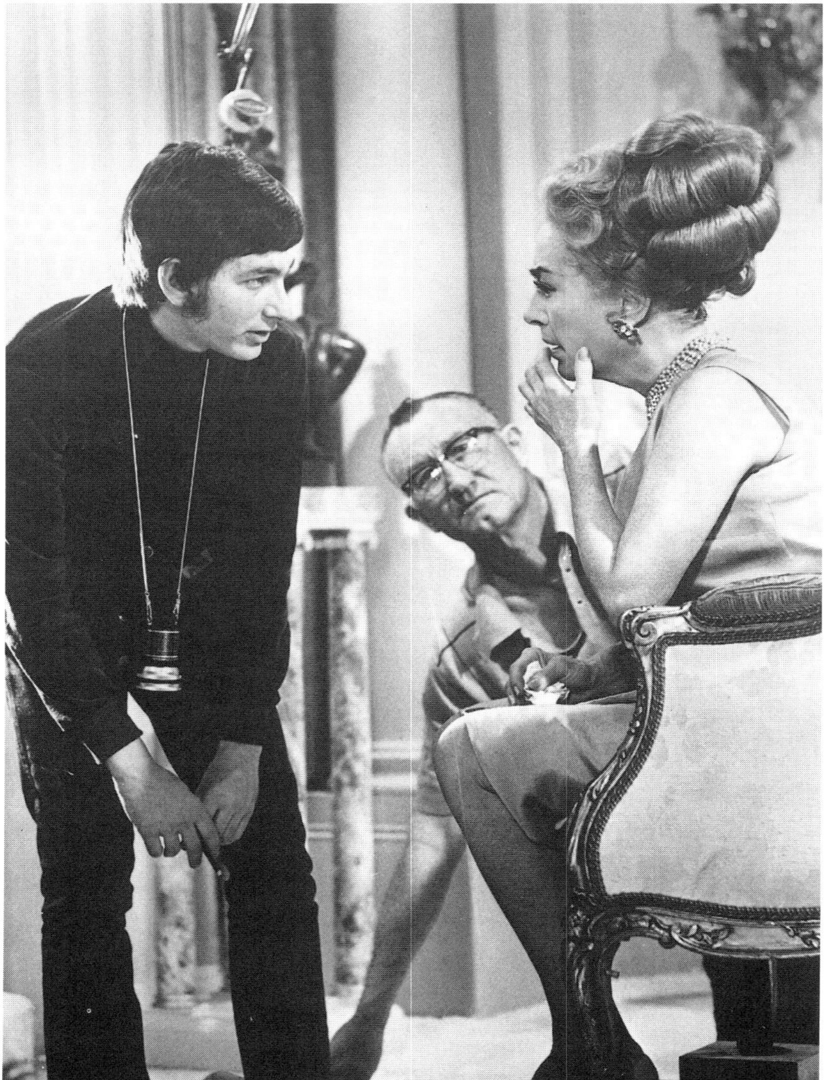

Steven directs Joan Crawford in the premiere episode of Night Gallery *(1969).* (Photofest)

Once on the soundstage, a nervous Spielberg had to prove himself to the experienced crew who were not used to working with such a young director. (At the time the still gawky Spielberg looked as if he was 15 years old.) Anxious to earn the technicians' approval and cooperation, he set up elaborate visual shots, hoping to dazzle his coworkers with his technique. However, he quickly was ordered by company executives to be less arty and more productive in getting the episode shot. Before long he was churning out more than 10 pages of script per day. In this on-the-job initiation, he also learned the necessity of being responsive to his cast's creative needs. In one case, an upset Crawford demanded that he provide her with several retakes of her crucial final moments on camera as she stumbles in the dark and tumbles through a window to her death. He did so, and the filming wound to a conclusion.

When *Night Gallery* aired in November 1969, Steven received mixed reviews for his contribution to what was, overall, an unoriginal movie. At Universal TV he was now regarded as a young-looking kid who was too absorbed with fancy camerawork. This reputation hindered him from getting new directing assignments. Fretting over his situation, he tried to interest the studio in producing several feature film ideas he had, but no one seemed interested. As the situation continued Steven grew despondent, and he asked for a leave of absence.

Thus, Sidney Sheinberg arranged for Spielberg to take time off from the studio.

Taking the Next Career Steps

During the last half of 1969 and into early 1970, Steven tried to raise financing to make his own low-budget feature films, but he was unsuccessful in his attempts. Thus he worked on screenplays with other writers in the hopes of generating a project at one of the big studios. One of these was *Ace Eli and Rodger of the Skies*. Set in the Midwest in the 1920s, the story concerns a barnstorming pilot who is having a difficult relationship with his adolescent son. Twentieth Century-Fox expressed interest in the tale and reluctantly agreed to consider letting Steven direct it. However, before a decision was made, a new set of producers took over the venture and they refused to have an inexperienced talent direct "their" film. However, the finished movie did not see release until 1973, when it failed at the box office. But it did provide Spielberg with his first official credit on a Hollywood feature film—as a story writer.

Once other studios began to show even a little professional interest in Steven, Universal renewed interest in their contract director. For his part, Spielberg was anxious to return to work, even if it was in television, which he regarded as second best to directing feature films. Forced into turning out one television episode after another, in 1970 to 1971 he guided segments of such small-screen series as *Marcus Welby, M.D.*, *The Name of the Game*, *Columbo*, and *Owen Marshall, Counselor at Law*.

While Spielberg was efficient and creative in handling these run-of-the-mill assignments, he was not happy undertaking such work. But even this artistically unsatisfying period proved useful for the young director. Television work allowed Steven the opportunity to season his skills and to experiment with his camera setups, try new sound edits, and test new approaches on how to involve the viewer in the action on-screen. Sometimes, when Spielberg was particularly dissatisfied with the quality of an episode script, he persuaded the show's producer to let him help with rewrites. Thus, these apprentice years were a good, if painful, training ground for him.

As his various TV projects aired, Steven began to receive better reviews. He was starting to make a name for himself in the Hollywood community. With his steady income, he moved away from the two-bedroom bungalow he shared with producer and friend Ralph Burris in Universal City. On his own, he took a house in the more prestigious Laurel Canyon area, a few miles away from Hollywood and Beverly Hills.

A Big Breakthrough

In summer 1971 Spielberg, who was always on the lookout for a script that he could develop into a screen showcase for himself, read the screenplay for *Duel*. He urged the movie's producer to let him handle the project. Then he attempted to get it made as a theatrical feature rather than the made-for-TV movie it was planned to be. That effort failed. No one of note was interested in starring in a seemingly simple story about an ordinary salesman who finds himself at the mercy of an unseen driver of a diesel truck on a lonely stretch of highway. Finally, Universal convinced Dennis Weaver, the star of its TV police series *McCloud*, to take the key role of the salesman.

Duel was filmed largely on a section of highway some 40 miles north of Los Angeles, and Steven had the benefit of working with an experienced crew. With their cooperation he devised creative methods to disguise the fact that much of the story action was taking place on the same used slice of roadway. Most important to the ultimate success of this project was Spielberg's insistence that neither the audience nor the hero ever see the story's menacing truck driver (beyond his arm sticking out the window). It increased the tension of this common man fighting for survival against an anonymous, but deadly, piece of machinery.

As the television movie was being rushed through editing to meet the November 13, 1971, airdate on ABC-TV, studio and network executives who saw cuts of the 73-minute feature were impressed with Spielberg's work. In an unusual step for a TV movie, the studio spent a good deal of money to publicize the film's premiere on televi-

Dennis Weaver in Duel *(1971).* (Photofest)

sion. When it aired, the reviews were highly complimentary. The entertainment trade paper *Daily Variety* said that the "film belongs on the classic shelf reserved for top suspensers."

Deciding to build on the fine reception *Duel* received, Universal had Spielberg shoot additional scenes to make the movie 90 minutes long. In this form it could be released as a full-length feature in foreign countries. As part of Universal's special promotion for the foreign distribution of *Duel,* Spielberg made his first trip outside of the country. In Europe and elsewhere the tightly constructed thriller was praised. It made the 25-year-old Steven an "immediate" success with the international film community.

Steven returned to Universal and directed two more TV movies: *Something Evil* (1972) and *Savage* (1973). Both movies had mediocre scripts, but Steven compensated for this by instilling the visuals and plot with his by-now trademark smart touches. However, one reviewer criticized *Something Evil* for its lack of "vivid emotional involvement." This was a criticism that would be leveled at Spielberg repeatedly over the coming years.

A Rocky Highway

Just as Sidney Sheinberg had guided Steven's directing career in the TV realm, so Jennings Lang proved a worthy benefactor of Spielberg in the area of theatrical features. Lang, a veteran talent agent who had become a movie producer, was a top executive in the Universal studio hierarchy. While working his way through TV assignments in the early 1970s, Steven came to know Lang, who was Sheinberg's mentor. Realizing the value of making new industry contacts and friendships, Spielberg developed close ties to Lang both on the lot and off, getting to know him and his family on a personal level.

Although he had been offered several directing assignments, in the spring of 1972 Steven wanted to make a picture about a true-life case in Texas. It involved a young couple on the run, who were desperate to rescue their baby from foster parents and avoid having the child put up for adoption. Spielberg presented the story idea to Lang who permitted him to team with a pair of screenwriters to develop the concept. The project, eventually known as *The Sugarland Express*, gained Lang's approval: It was given the green light (an industry term for a go-ahead) for a full script. However, the studio hierarchy changed its mind and put the potential film on hold indefinitely.

Then, just as suddenly, Universal renewed its interest in the property when the production team of Richard D. Zanuck and David Brown joined the studio under a multiple film deal. The duo had already met Spielberg a few years earlier when he pitched his *Ace Eli and Rodger of the Skies* screenplay to them at Twentieth Century-Fox. The producers eventually agreed to let Steven direct *The Sugarland Express*.

Similar to *Duel*, *The Sugarland Express* was a road picture with a twist: A reckless, young couple on their way to Sugarland, Texas, to grab their child from the authorities, kidnap a sheriff. In the process, a convoy of police vehicles chases the young bandits. Because Spielberg was still relatively new at professional filmmaking—and this was his first true theatrical feature—he was quite open to suggestions from fellow talent. Cinematographer Vilmos

Zsigmond, who filmed this picture, said, "Steven gave me a 100 percent chance to collaborate. . . . He asked the impossible with a smile on his face. How could you say no?"

Shot largely on location in Texas, Spielberg overcame all the obstacles of filming the intricate and lengthy car chase that was the centerpiece of the picture. At the same time he did his best to make the characters the primary focus. His greatest challenge, however, was to avoid having the movie become too comedic. This was a distinct possibility because the producers had cast Goldie Hawn, an actress known primarily for comedic roles, as a lead in the film.

When released in 1974, *The Sugarland Express* was not a commercial success. Audiences expected it would be a lighthearted Hawn movie (the type for which she was typically known), and moviegoers were disappointed by the film's mix of comedy, serious overtones, and (in the second half of the picture) a downbeat turn of events which leads to a tragic ending. At least Spielberg had the consolation of receiving several flattering reviews. Pauline Kael, of the *New Yorker,* lavishly praised the effort as "one of the most phenomenal debut films in the history of movies." But such admiration did not satisfy Steven. As he told *Newsweek* magazine, his goal was to make pictures that "appeal to millions of people," not "small critical successes nobody goes to see."

Spielberg (right) works with William Atherton and Goldie Hawn on the set of The Sugarland Express *(1973).* (Photofest)

Pursuing a "Razor-Sharp" Opportunity

After Spielberg completed *The Sugarland Express,* he had a realization: "I've discovered I've got this preoccupation with ordinary people pursued by large forces. A personal movie for me is one about people with obsessions."

Jaws certainly fit that mold. Spielberg had seen a copy of the soon-to-be published Peter Benchley novel in the offices of Richard D. Zanuck and David Brown. After reading it, Steven expressed to several producers his interest in directing the thriller. At this point, the executives were pleased with the footage Steven had shot on (the not-yet-released) *The Sugarland Express*. However, because of the huge technical problems involved in filming the shark-versus-man story of *Jaws,* they initially felt a more seasoned director was needed for the film. But after meeting with a few veteran directors, Zanuck and Brown agreed that what the complicated movie needed was a fresh approach to the story. They decided to take another chance on the enthusiastic young Spielberg.

Having won his campaign to direct *Jaws*, Spielberg had second thoughts. He feared that making this picture could label him as a director only capable of handling stories about trucks and sharks. After much debate, in mid 1973, he contracted to do the picture. Less than a year later he was at work directing *Jaws* on Martha's Vineyard, a resort island off the coast of Massachusetts.

Casting the "shark movie" was difficult, especially filling the role of the young ichthyologist (a scientist who studies fish). Jon Voight and others turned down the screen part, fearing they would be overshadowed by the vicious title character. Another actor, Richard Dreyfuss, also said no to the role. He insisted, "I'd rather watch this movie than shoot it." However, Spielberg's enthusiasm and confidence eventually won Dreyfuss over. It was the start of a long and successful working relationship between director and actor, and Steven soon regarded Richard as his other half, his "alter ego."

Overcoming Production Obstacles

Not yet content with the screenplay, which had already gone through several drafts, Spielberg wanted rewrites. He discarded subplots from the original novel and focused on the exciting aspects of the hunt for the monster "who just chows down." On the other hand, he was careful not to play up too much the story line's existing similarities to Herman Melville's classic novel *Moby-Dick*, fearing it would make his movie seem like a rehash of that famous story. One of Steven's many personal touches to the story—based on his outlook on life and his strong urge to please audiences—was to alter the book's ending. Instead of having Dreyfuss's hippie scientist character die in the final encounter with the fiendish shark as he did in the book, he survives the climactic battle.

Adding to the complexity of the already difficult shoot was the mechanical shark required for key sequences within *Jaws*. In this era before sophisticated computer-generated special effects, three of the sharks were specially constructed on the West Coast and then shipped by truck to the East Coast. Each proved to be disastrous when put to the test: One exploded, one sank, and the third just wouldn't function properly during filming. While the remaining mechanical beast—known as "Bruce"—was tinkered with by its special-effects designer, Steven continued filming.

Not having the mechanical shark available through most of the filming proved beneficial to the picture. Without this important prop, Spielberg had to rethink creatively many of the planned camera setups involving the shark. Thus, in many scenes in *Jaws*, the killer shark's presence is felt rather than actually seen. As with *Duel*, this psychological point of view heightened the on-screen sense of terror. Now moviegoers could bring their own vivid imaginations into full play while watching the picture. This made the perceived terror that much greater and very exciting.

Besides the unpredictable weather during location shooting, there was also the problem of dealing with tourists who either accidentally or purposely got in the way of the filming. (One "extra" who received special treatment was Spielberg's father, who visited the Martha's Vineyard location and was persuaded to be on camera in a crowd scene on the beach.) As obstacles and setbacks mounted, the *Jaws* shoot fell farther and farther behind schedule. Many times Steven wished he could abandon the troubled project, but it would have badly damaged his industry reputation to do so. Both of Spielberg's mentors—

Sidney Sheinberg and Jennings Lang—at different points during production had to convince Spielberg not to quit the project. Worried Universal executives frequently visited the East Coast set and wondered aloud why such an

Knee-deep in a delayed production schedule and ocean water, Spielberg often thought of leaving the Jaws *project.* (Photofest)

action picture should be going so far over its schedule and initial budget.

By now this jinxed production was being called *Flaws* by its exasperated cast and crew, who badly wanted to return home to their families as well as to other professional commitments. Toughened by the constant strain of filming obstacles every day, Steven had become obsessed with not only completing the picture, but also completing the thriller exactly as he envisioned it. He proved to be a stern taskmaster to all involved in the shoot.

Back in Los Angeles, after wrap-up filming in a studio tank and at nearby Catalina Island, *Jaws* went into postproduction. This part of the filmmaking process includes picture editing, sound editing, dialogue retakes, music scoring, adding in visual effects, as well as making release prints and preparing materials to promote the picture. During this time, the contributions of two craftspeople proved extremely helpful to the success of *Jaws*. Veteran film editor Verna Fields worked on the footage to heighten the pacing and balance of scenes, and movie composer John Williams created a pulsating score, which included the highly effective simple shark theme that has become a classic.

A Huge Success

After positive prerelease test screenings in various U.S. cities, *Jaws* premiered in June 1975. It became a smash hit, as word-of-mouth of the thrilling (even frightening) screen escapade spread from moviegoer to moviegoer. So enormous was the public reaction to *Jaws* that its financial success did much to alter the way the Hollywood industry viewed the making and releasing of feature films. From the example of Spielberg's *Jaws*, industry executives learned that instead of opening a movie in a few major cities and then showing it later in other locations, a movie could be successfully screened at many locations throughout the country simultaneously.

Jaws was a trend-setting film in several other ways, as well. It led to a greater appreciation for the value and profitability of merchandise licensing agreements involving movie tie-in products, which, in this case, ranged from T-shirts to inflatable sharks. With *Jaws*, Hollywood also began to realize possibilities for movie franchises, that is, several movie sequels could be produced from a hit blockbuster picture, and a large portion of fans of the first film would return for the follow-ups. (In the case of *Jaws*, there would be three big-screen sequels, none of which Spielberg chose to direct.)

When the final tallies were in, *Jaws*, which had cost $12 million to make, grossed $470.6 million in worldwide distribution. It became the highest grossing film released to that date. Like any filmmaking venture, *Jaws* was a highly collaborative effort, but Steven received most of the credit for this box-office bonanza, which one reviewer smartly

Spielberg and the shark that made him famous. (Photofest)

labeled "a perfect money machine." Despite the great reviews, what Spielberg most wanted was to win an Academy Award for his directing achievements on *Jaws*.

When the Oscars nominations were announced in February 1976, Spielberg was shaken to learn that he was not in the running for the Best Director award. (*Jaws* was nominated in categories of Editing, Music, Sound, and Best Picture, and would win in the first three of these fields.) Regaining his composure from this industry slap in the face, Steven said with forced lightness: "When a film makes a lot of money, people resent it. Everybody loves a winner. But nobody loves a *winner*."

When a filmmaker has an enormous box-office success such as Spielberg did with *Jaws*, the film industry often wonders how quickly this burst of fame will swell the young director's head. In actuality, in the wake of *Jaws'* success, Steven had periods when he thought the film had been a "fluke." He said, "I began believing it was some kind of freak and agreeing when people said it could never happen again."

Despite his doubts, Spielberg was pleased that he had achieved his artistic vision of making *Jaws* a visual thrill, a shock, and a fear ride that many moviegoers had obviously enjoyed. Connecting with and winning the approval of millions of people through his films was a way for him to overcome his difficult childhood as an outsider.

With the stellar response to *Jaws,* Steven also earned millions of dollars and a highly bankable name in Hollywood. With this new and profitable reputation, he was able to persuade Columbia Pictures to expand the budget for his next project: *Close Encounters of the Third Kind.*

4

THE SUPERSTAR FILMMAKER

Although nearly 30 years old, Steven Spielberg still looked boyish in the mid-1970s, despite that he had grown up quickly in the movie industry. He had learned the importance of making good contacts (also known as networking) within the business, and he had come to appreciate the value of expanding his interests. Thus, when it came to making *Close Encounters of the Third Kind*, he moved away from Universal and tried his "luck" at another studio. In this instance, he picked Columbia Pictures, one of the movie companies bidding for Spielberg's services. Everyone speculated whether the gifted filmmaker would bring the same box-office magic to his new production as he did to *Jaws*.

Steven on the set in the late 1970s. (Photofest)

Creating His Epic

Alienated from the mainstream in his childhood, Spielberg had easily related to the aliens who were so often the subject of the science-fiction movies he thrived on seeing in the 1950s. It was this sense of kinship that had drawn him to making his amateur movie, *Firelight*, in 1964. Now, more than a decade later, he reworked the story idea into the elaborate *Close Encounters of the Third Kind,* which, at first, was called *Watch the Skies*. Unlike *Jaws*, which he regarded as a "big fish story" and "a methodical attempt to manipulate an audience," *Close Encounters of the Third Kind* was a personal film, based on his own idea and screenplay.

Unlike his youthful *Firelight* in which the presentation did not always make it clear as to the good or bad intentions of the space visitors, Steven now had a clearer approach. Rather than follow the usual Hollywood concept that creatures from outer space are the sworn enemy of mankind, Spielberg held the opposite view. He was more in agreement with the offbeat sci-fi entry, *The Day the Earth Stood Still* (1951). In this, one of his favorite movies, the aliens are presented as essentially kind, mentally advanced individuals who come to Earth in peace and goodwill. Given Steven's own traumatic childhood, it is understandable why he would connect emotionally with helpful extraterrestrials who are misunderstood by suspicious earthlings.

Since motion pictures (especially those seen in childhood) created much of Spielberg's frame of reference in life, into the plot of his new epic he worked imagery from two favorite moments of old Walt Disney movies: the terrifying, furious "Night on Bald Mountain" episode from *Fantasia* and the reassuring "When You Wish Upon a Star" sequence and song from *Pinocchio*. Because these cinema references were from two popular and frequently seen pictures, he felt certain that a large number of moviegoers had shared a similar response to this screen footage. Such shrewd assumptions were part of the genius touch that made Spielberg's movies so easy for audiences to respond to and appreciate.

Although Steven would receive sole credit for *Close Encounters*' screenplay, others (including Paul Schrader) collaborated on the script, adding touches over a two-year period that began while *Jaws* was in production. The new project revolved around the public's ongoing fascination with whether unidentified flying objects (UFOs) were a reality. The film's title was derived from UFO terminology. An encounter of the first kind is any sighting of a UFO. The second level includes tangible evidence that UFOs—and extraterrestrials—really do exist. The third kind is actual physical contact as well as definite communication with alien beings.

Spielberg's plot involves an average family man who encounters a UFO during a mysterious blackout in rural Indiana. The electric company linesman shares this experience with a stranger and her young son, whom he meets during the power shortage. Together they witness small UFOs flying overhead. Thereafter, the hero is convinced that outer space visitors will arrive on Earth in their mother ship and that he must make contact with them. He abandons his family to undertake his mission, joined by the woman he met, who is now searching desperately for her missing boy who was whisked off in a spacecraft. Along with others, they overcome government interference and other obstacles to connect with the forces aboard the now-landed spaceship. Soon the vanished youngster is among those released by the aliens, who communicate that they have come in peace. Later, the obsessed linesman is among the team who join the aliens aboard their spacecraft.

Bringing His Vision to Life

In shaping the screenplay, Steven had a primary focus: "I really wanted to take a child's point of view." In particular, that youngster was Spielberg himself. When one of the director's sisters, Sue, read the screenplay, she had a strong emotional reaction to the text. "There was so much of our childhood in that film—scenes of the children fighting and the parents fighting. When I saw it I burst out into tears." It reminded Sue of the awful quarrels that her parents had undergone in the years before they finally divorced.

Once more, Spielberg chose Richard Dreyfuss to play the lead role and be the filmmaker's alter ego in the new release. Steven selected French film director François Truffaut, one of his moviemaker idols, to play the sympathetic scientist. Vilmos Zsigmond, who had worked on *The Sugarland Express,* was again the cinematographer. Like many film directors—especially with elaborate, special-

Richard Dreyfuss in his leading role in Close Encounters of the Third Kind. (Photofest)

effects-heavy projects—Steven relied heavily on the use of storyboards, which are a series of drawings, or sometimes photographs, depicting the progression of shots in a movie sequence. However, much as he tried to preplan each step of the complex shoot, he would frequently get new ideas from watching a movie the night before filming a scene, and it would inspire fresh thoughts of how to better his project.

One of the more difficult aspects of making *Close Encounters* was directing the actors in sequences that would later have special effects added to the visuals. It was tough for Spielberg to convey properly to the actors what they should imagine they were seeing on the soundstage so they could react properly on camera. At such times Spielberg had to disguise his own uncertainty of how these special effects (under the direction of Douglas Trumbull) would eventually materialize. For a man of Steven's nature who wanted total control of a situation, such qualms about how the special effects would turn out—in comparison to his own vision—must have been difficult to endure.

Actual production on *Close Encounters of the Third Kind* began in May 1976, but its completion kept extending as Spielberg's vision continued to expand day by day. In the process, the film's budget rose from $4.1 million to an eventual $20 million. It required great faith on the studio's part and constant reassurances from Spielberg that the end results of this effort would justify what were then very high costs.

Because so much of *Close Encounters* depended upon its special effects, the postproduction process was long, complicated, and exceedingly expensive. Looking for better methods to produce these crucial visuals, Steven tested computer-generated imagery (CGI). However, that technology was still in its infancy and was bypassed for more traditional means.

The climactic spaceship arrival in Close Encounters of the Third Kind. (Literature/Film Archive)

Once again, Spielberg collaborated with composer John Williams on the film's score. Just as Williams had devised

a distinctive motif for the shark in *Jaws*, he did so for their new film. For his original score, Williams fashioned a five-note theme used as the means of communication between the scientists on Earth and the visitors on board the mother ship. It set a memorable tone for the entire movie.

Ready for Release

Close Encounters of the Third Kind was not ready for distribution until November 1977. Once it hit theaters, the reviews were full of praise. *Time* magazine judged that this new entry "offers proof, if any were needed, that Spielberg's reputation is no accident. His new movie is richer than *Jaws*, and it reaches the viewer at a far more profound level than *Star Wars*." Many other critics responded equally favorably to

Steven's optimistic, imaginative story and commented on the picture's key scene. In that unforgettable footage, the curious boy (played by Cary Guffey) is attracted by an overwhelmingly intense light (from an alien craft). He calmly opens the door to his house and walks without fear into the bright illumination. This highly emotional sequence became one of the signature scenes in Spielberg's body of film work.

In worldwide distribution, *Close Encounters* grossed a massive $300 million. It was nominated for eight Academy Awards, including Steven's first nomination for Best Director, and it won the Oscar for Best Cinematography. Disappointed again at not winning the Academy Award for directing, Spielberg insisted that claiming such a trophy was not "the last goal" for him.

Even after its release, the doors did not shut on *Close Encounters*. Spielberg had been unhappy that the studio had rushed him to meet their release date for this expensive entry and had not permitted him to further tinker with his "baby." In subsequent months, he convinced Columbia Pictures to let him shoot additional sequences and incorporate new special effects to produce a special edition of *Close Encounters of the Third Kind,* which was released in 1979. In the process, he edited out several minutes of original footage and reinserted several scrapped outtakes. This time around, he focused the movie's climax on providing audiences with a glimpse inside of the mother ship.

A Creative Misfire

While making *Close Encounters of the Third Kind* in 1976, Spielberg met actress Amy Irving, who was 22. She had made her feature film debut that year in the horror thriller *Carrie*. The daughter of an actress and a TV director/producer, she and Steven began dating and soon were living together. At the time, each was fearful of sacrificing his or her career to domesticity and they avoided marriage.

Meanwhile, Spielberg rejected directing the sequel to *Jaws* because the studio would not approve his story ideas. Thus Jeannot Szwarc directed the first sequel in 1978, with other filmmakers handling the next two installments. Instead, Steven involved himself in the making of a movie comedy. It was not a simple, lighthearted story, but a big-budgeted farce dealing with his favorite time period—the 1940s. He loves this period in history, Spielberg says, because "it was naive and it was somewhat innocent and it represented the growing pains of the 20th century. And it's a very fertile time for movie stories."

His new picture, *1941*, was based on real-life events that occurred in southern California during World War II in the months following Japan's sneak attack on Pearl Harbor in Hawaii. As the plot unfolds, due to a chain of misunderstandings the U.S. military thinks enemy planes are flying over Los Angeles. They respond to the situation with a lengthy barrage from antiaircraft guns before discovering their error.

John Belushi (left) and Toshiro Mifune in 1941 *(1979), one of Spielberg's less successful efforts.* (Literature/Film Archive)

What started out as a nearly $12 million creation made as a joint venture between Universal and Columbia studios, soon mushroomed into a $35 million lead balloon filled with miscast talent, including John Belushi and Dan Aykroyd. Steven explained later, "We went from one plot to seven subplots. But at the time, I wanted it—the bigness, the power, hundreds of people at my beck and call, millions of dollars at my disposal, and everybody saying, Yes, yes, yes." Long before the picture finished production he realized that the results on screen were hardly funny and that comedy, at least at this point in his career, was definitely *not* his strong point. Despite the reshuffling of scenes, the restructuring of special effects, and other editing, the movie was, in the view of Steven's mentor Sidney Sheinberg, "a mess." When the film debuted in late 1979, one Los Angeles newspaper critic described *1941* as "a movie that will live in infamy."

Eventually—thanks to a better reception abroad than in the United States—the unwieldy film turned a profit. But by then the artistic failure had been perceived in Hollywood as a box-office loser that tarnished Steven's golden image. As he observed (even before the film was released), "I can see *1941* as a cleansing experience. The one possible way I can make you forget all the good things I've done in motion pictures."

Spielberg was so sure that *1941* would flop that he was too embarrassed to remain in Los Angeles for its premiere.

Instead, that December he and Amy Irving, who were now engaged, flew to Japan on what was to be their honeymoon. Unfortunately, during the trip, the couple had a serious argument and separated. An emotionally shaken Steven returned alone to California.

Bouncing Back

During the 1970s, Spielberg had made many film industry friends. One of his closest was fellow moviemaker George Lucas. After Lucas enjoyed a phenomenal success in 1977 with his science-fiction epic *Star Wars*, Steven suggested that he would love to direct one of the sequels that was sure to spring from this massive box-office hit. That idea did not fly with Lucas, who had his own vision for the movie series. However, Lucas suggested that the two come up with a lively action adventure modeled after the movie serials of the 1930s and 1940s. This was the springboard for *Raiders of the Lost Ark*. Both Steven and George contributed story ideas for the project, which was scripted by Lawrence Kasdan. Lucas served as one of the film's executive producers, while Spielberg directed the big-budgeted Paramount Pictures release.

Lucas, who was essentially in financial control of the movie, persuaded Spielberg to use many of the British crew—and even locations—that been employed for *Star Wars* and its 1979 sequel, *The Empire Strikes Back*.

George Lucas (left) and Spielberg, both superstar creators of action and fantasy films, collaborated on 1981's Raiders of the Lost Ark. (Photofest)

Harrison Ford, who played Hans Solo in the *Star Wars* films, was cast in the lead part of Indiana Jones, the globe-trotting professor and adventurer in search of a much-wanted religious artifact. Originally, Amy Irving was to play Indiana's female companion on his death-defying adventures. However, after she and Spielberg parted, the assignment went to actress Karen Allen, who appeared in *National Lampoon's Animal House*.

Spielberg never felt emotionally close to *Raiders of the Lost Ark* over the course of its 16-week shooting schedule. He sometimes questioned whether he or Lucas had ultimate responsibility for this overgrown boy's escapade filled with often violent action. Lucas was sometimes present for the day-to-day filming, and there were occasions when the two Hollywood pals disagreed on the proper approach and tone for the picture. In a much-quoted exchange, George joked, "Well, it's your movie. If the audience doesn't like it, they're going to blame you." Steven responded, "Okay, but I'm going to tell them that *you* made me do it."

At a later time, Spielberg would recall, "While I was doing *Raiders* I felt I was losing touch with the reason I became a moviemaker—to make stories about people and relationships." Not feeling personally attached to the entry and thus not insistent on constantly expanding its initial guidelines, Steven completed the project slightly under budget ($20.4 million) and 12 days less than the announced shooting schedule of 85 days.

Released in June 1981, *Raiders of the Lost Ark* grossed a whopping $384 million in worldwide distribution and won several Oscar nominations (including one for Spielberg's direction). It earned four Academy Awards (including Best Sound and Best Editing), but Steven again lost out in the directing category.

Gaining New Steam

Although he dated other women after his traumatic separation from Amy Irving, Spielberg was still emotionally at loose ends during the making of *Raiders of the Lost Ark*. It led him to thinking, "What I really need is a friend I can talk to—somebody who can give me *all* the answers." Caught in this train of thought, he focused on the alien visitors who popped in and out of *Close Encounters of the Third Kind*. It prompted him to speculate, "What if I were 10 years old again—where I've sort of been for 34 years anyway—and what if he [the extraterrestrial] needed me as much as I needed him?" Entranced with this notion, he asked, "Wouldn't that be a great love story?"

These ideas melded with thoughts for a new science-fiction movie he wanted to direct based on a script called *Night Skies* by John Sayles. Abandoning the Sayles screenplay, Spielberg instead chose to make *E.T. the Extra-*

Terrestrial. Because Sayles was busy with his own directing projects, he could not help with the new concept. Screenwriter Melissa Mathison then stepped into the picture. Exchanging ideas back and forth with Spielberg, Mathison wrote a screenplay about a kindly visitor from outer space stranded on Earth when his spaceship leaves without him. Universal agreed to distribute the film.

E.T. is one of Spielberg's most personal films. It reflects many of his childhood wishes ("I used to imagine strange creatures lurking outside my bedroom window, and I'd wish that they'd come into my life and magically change it"). It also mirrors his youthful feelings of being an outsider while living in suburbia. Most of all it represents the anxieties he suffered as a youngster when his parents were heading toward divorce and he felt increasingly abandoned by them. (In *E.T.* the boy's father has recklessly run off with another woman, leaving the 10-year-old's distraught mother to care for her children.)

E.T. also revealed an emotional maturing within the filmmaker. In *Close Encounters of the Third Kind* the lead character abandons his family to pursue his fascination with the outer space visitors. In *E.T.*, the little boy realizes that his oddly shaped extraterrestrial pal must accompany his own kind back to their distant planet while he, the Earthling, belongs on Earth with his relatives. This sharp contrast between the two science-fiction pictures echoed Spielberg's growing personal desire to have a stable family life of his own and to take a more optimistic view toward life.

Creating Screen Magic

Budgeted at a relatively modest $10.5 million, Spielberg knew that in *E.T.* he must draw believable performances from two of the key child actors: the preteen Elliott and his younger sister Gertie. In choosing Henry Thomas and Drew Barrymore, respectively, for these major assignments he was extremely fortunate. Each gave natural, endearing performances. Steven, who had never lost his own connection with childhood, was well equipped to communicate effectively with his juvenile performers. According to Spielberg, "I felt the best way to work with Henry [Thomas] in *E.T.* was not to be his director, but his buddy." As part of this approach, the filmmaker spent most lunch hours during production playing video games (one of his own passions) with his young talent.

Years later Drew Barrymore recalled of the *E.T.* director, "When I had to cry, he was amazing. He had this special way of talking to you and his voice would change and it made you cry. There was something so gentle about it." She also remembered Spielberg's fun-loving side. For example, "On Halloween we were to dress up. Steven was a woman and he directed all day in the woman's costume. He looked great!"

Spielberg became good friends with Henry Thomas on the set of E.T. *(1982).* (Photofest)

The other pivotal figure in *E.T.* was the strangely shaped, lovable title character. He was the delightful figure with the potbelly, the oversized head (with protruding eyes) on a long, stringy neck, and those magical fingers—including the digit that glowed. Having designed alien figures for *Close Encounters,* Carlo Rambaldi was called upon to provide the various E.T.s used for the new filming: an electronic figure, a puppet that could walk, and a special E.T. costume to be worn by various small actors. What made the combination of these three versions come so wonderfully to life was the cinematography of Allen

Daviau. He had worked with Spielberg years before on two short subjects (the unfinished *Slipstream* and *Amblin'*) and the director had never forgotten his talents.

Adding emotional strength to the 115-minute screen fantasy was John Williams's effective music score. It was equally appropriate both in sounding E.T's special melodic theme and in the movie's highlight sequence. In that scene, another classic Spielberg moment, Elliott and the other youngsters are helping E.T. flee from government agents who want to keep the alien on Earth in order to study him, not knowing that the Earth's atmosphere will eventually kill the creature. With E.T. safely in Elliott's bicycle handlebar basket, he and his young helpers peddle their bikes furiously and rise magically into the air. It is a liberating, highly emotional sequence.

Except in shooting scenes involving complicated special effects, Steven avoided his standard practice of using storyboards to help organize his directing chores. He realized that in order to gain the needed naturalness from his young cast, he had to allow them and himself to improvise. By permitting himself such flexibility Spielberg gave the performers the necessary breathing space to make their interpretations free-flowing and unaffected. It was a technique that he would utilize frequently in the coming years.

When *E.T. the Extra-Terrestrial* debuted in June 1982, Spielberg proved that he indeed had his finger on the

Spielberg chats with his out-of-this-world friend and star of E.T. (© Mark Sennet/Reflex/Photofest)

pulse of the world's filmgoing public. The film grossed a spectacular $701 million in worldwide distribution. Besides winning critical endorsements from most reviewers, Steven won his third Academy Award nomination for Best Director, but once again he did not win the award. His film, however, went on to win four Oscars, including Best Music Score.

By comparison, audience response to *E.T.* around the globe dwarfed the highly impressive receptions of *Jaws* and *Close Encounters*. With its huge merchandizing campaign, *E.T.* was licensed for a wide range of products, including the candy used in the film's story, dolls, and even alien-shaped telephones. The media attention devoted to *E.T.* resulted in Spielberg becoming the movie guru of the early 1980s. His fame reached such a peak that he became a household name—a rarity for film directors. He was in such demand that he even attended a special White House screening of *E.T.* for President and Mrs. Reagan.

At age 35, Steven Spielberg had become the king of Hollywood.

5

A TURBULENT AND PRODUCTIVE DECADE

Once Steven Spielberg gained fame with *Duel* and *Jaws*, aspiring moviemakers—some still in film school—began flocking to him for such advice as how to break into the film industry and how to get their projects made into theatrical releases. Throughout the 1980s and beyond, Spielberg has often become deeply involved in producing other directors' motion pictures and serving as a mentor to the next generation of filmmakers.

New Roles and New Lessons

As executive producer, Steven gave input to such feature films as the nostalgic *I Wanna Hold Your Hand* (1978) and the comedy *Used Cars* (1980), both directed by Robert Zemeckis. For 1982's *Poltergeist*, directed by Tobe Hooper (famous for his horror entry *The Texas Chainsaw Massacre*), Spielberg was producer, supplied the story, and cowrote the screenplay, much of which was inspired by his childhood fears and fantasies.

During production of *Poltergeist* Spielberg spent so much time on the sets, and participated so extensively in the decision-making, that word spread in Hollywood that Steven was as much the director of the picture as was Hooper. This complicated situation put each man in an uncomfortable position within the industry. As a result of the controversy (about who was the picture's real director), Steven made a decision about his moviemaking path: "If I write it myself, I'll direct it myself." (Spielberg did not participate in the two *Poltergeist* sequels made in the 1980s.)

During this period Spielberg functioned as almost a one-man film factory, and a new mentor, Steve Ross, guided him in his professional path. Ross was the chairman of the board of Time Warner, the company that owned the Warner Bros. studio. From their first meeting in 1981 until Ross's death in 1992, the two industry figures were close friends and tightly bound business associates. This led Steven into making several of his pictures for Warner Bros., and he learned much from his high-level tutor about the finesse required to become a true film-industry giant.

In 1982, Steven was involved in a tragedy-plagued movie. He and friend John Landis, the director of such hit comedies as *National Lampoon's Animal House* and *The Blue Brothers*, teamed to produce *The Twilight Zone—the Motion Picture*. The script was based on episodes from Rod Serling's old TV series (*The Twilight Zone*), with Landis and Spielberg each directing a segment, and two other directors (Joe Dante and George Miller) handling the other two. (Landis also provided a prologue tying the four episodes together.) During production of Landis's main installment, a tragic accident occurred on the sound stage that killed veteran actor Vic Morrow as well as two children who had been hired as extras. It led to a high-profile, lengthy court case that eventually cleared Landis and others who were in charge of the set that fatal evening of any overt criminal wrongdoing.

The in-production calamity cast a gloom not only on the film itself but also on the entire Hollywood community. Although it was demonstrated that Spielberg was never directly involved in the events that caused the fatalities during the filming, it was a tremendously sobering experience for Steven.

A Transitional Period

Continuing to expand his show business vision, in 1984 Steven and two frequent coworkers, Frank Marshall and

Harrison Ford, Ke Huy Quan, and Kate Capshaw go for a thrill ride in Indiana Jones and the Temple of Doom *(1984).* (Photofest)

Kathleen Kennedy (she having first worked for Spielberg as a secretary), formed Amblin Entertainment. Using his new company—located in a special complex on the Universal studio lot—as his base, Steven produced such films as *Gremlins* (1984) and 1985's *Goonies* (for which he also provided the story).

Often, when filmmakers become too successful in Hollywood, they are subjected to criticism—just or unjust—from within the movie industry. In Steven's case, it was theorized that he was a wonderful director of "light" entertainment (often termed popcorn movies) but that he was incapable of leading serious screen subjects. This seemed to be reaffirmed when he chose to direct 1984's *Indiana Jones and the Temple of Doom*, a prequel to *Raiders of the Lost Ark*. Again collaborating with George Lucas, they devised a nonstop action adventure once again starring Harrison Ford as the dashing and daring Indiana Jones. This time actress Kate Capshaw played the leading lady.

Raising the stakes on the slam-bang action and cliffhanger situations, the 118-minute feature was filled with nasty villains and gory situations. Although this entry proved exceedingly successful at the box office (grossing nearly $180 million in just domestic distribution), the picture's excessive violence upset many reviewers and moviegoers. In retrospect, Spielberg agreed that, given the young target audience for the film, he had overdone the gruesome aspects. He admitted that, in the process, he had learned his lesson and would be more restrained in the future.

During the casting of *Indiana Jones and the Temple of Doom*, Steven and leading lady Kate Capshaw had shared a brief, initial emotional attraction for one another. Nothing immediate, however, developed from the situation. She realized that he was still pining for his lost love, Amy Irving, who was busy pursuing her acting career. Later, when Spielberg flew to India to select colorful locations for his new action entry, he was surprised to find

Irving, then working in that country on a TV miniseries, on hand to greet him at the airport. The couple renewed their romantic relationship. Before long, Amy was pregnant with Steven's child. In November 1985, five months after the birth of their son Max, Spielberg and Irving married. Thrilled at becoming a family man, the filmmaker blossomed emotionally and spiritually as a husband and father.

A Serious Film from Spielberg

In what seemed a striking career move away from popcorn movies, Steven agreed to direct 1985's *The Color Purple*. It was based on Alice Walker's celebrated, controversial novel of life among African-Americans in the South of the early 20th century. Initially, Spielberg, a Jewish white man, seemed an odd choice to guide this sensitive story of a black woman abused by the black men in her painful life. However, Steven had loved Walker's book. He related deeply to its sensitive lead character, Celie, who awakens to her self-worth and eventually finds contentment.

What convinced Spielberg to proceed with the cinematic venture was a question asked by Quincy Jones (the black composer, musician, and entrepreneur who coproduced *The Color Purple*). Jones pointedly asked Spielberg, "You didn't have to come from Mars to do *E.T.* did you?"

Later, when Steven met with author Walker, she was impressed by his enthusiasm for her writing and his sincerity about translating her book onto the screen. She sensed that, because Spielberg's own painful childhood was still so with him, he would relate to the unhappy Celie, torn away from her own family and forced into years of heartache.

In casting *The Color Purple* Spielberg turned to several talented members of the African-American acting community, including Danny Glover, who was cast as the highly abusive Mister. Steven also made less obvious hiring choices. Alice Walker, among others, suggested that Spielberg consider Whoopi Goldberg, a stand-up comedian who had made a name for herself with her one-woman show. When Goldberg auditioned, she performed her stage act. Unable to contain her outrageous inner self, Whoopi included in her presentation a special skit she had devised based on *E.T. the Extra-Terrestrial*. Rather than be offended by Goldberg's spoof of his film, Steven was highly amused and impressed by Goldberg's talents. He offered her the lead role of Celie in *The Color Purple*.

Quincy Jones referred Oprah Winfrey to Steven for the assignment of Sofia, a secondary but important figure in the story. Jones had been visiting Chicago and had happened to tune into Winfrey's local TV talk show. He was impressed by her presence and her strong personality.

Spielberg chose Whoopi Goldberg, a stand-up comedian, to play the dramatic lead in The Color Purple *(1985).* (Photofest)

Although Oprah had never acted in a film, she gave a solid audition for Spielberg and was soon hired to play the proud character of Sophia.

Much of *The Color Purple* was shot in the small town of Marshville, North Carolina. As with *E.T.*, Spielberg chose not to rely on storyboards (except in the African sequences) to guide his daily filmmaking. Steven reasoned, "I wanted to surprise myself through the process of discovery every day during the making of the movie. I was afraid the storyboards would tie me down to preconceived ideas."

During the eight weeks of filming in the South, Spielberg devoted much of his time to guiding Whoopi through her pivotal acting task. According to Goldberg, who was making her movie debut, "Steven made it very easy for me to make the transition [to the screen]. He would say, 'There are 8 million mute people in this [camera] box here. They're all in one room looking through a one-way mirror; you can't see them, but they see you. They're mute, so you can't hear them, but they hear you, and they enjoy what you're doing.' And that's how the camera became my friend."

Dealing with Controversy

As *The Color Purple* went through its postproduction phase in the fall of 1985, a controversy grew over its forthcoming release. Some of the strongest opposition came from a Los Angeles-based organization called the Coalition Against Black Exploitation, which claimed, "The elevation of Alice Walker's book to the status of a movie will be devastating to the black community." The group particularly objected to the "degradation of the black male" (which Spielberg made even more one-dimensional and unfavorably presented than in the novel) and "the subtle promotion of lesbianism as an alternative to failed heterosexual relationships." (In actuality, Spielberg downplayed this aspect of the book in his film.) Other factions of the black community followed suit and criticized the making of the film for its possible furthering of African-American stereotypes.

Whoopi Goldberg, star of the film, came to Spielberg's defense in this storm of protest. She insisted that *The Color Purple* was "not about blacks. It's not even about sexism. It's about a search for self." As to why a Caucasian was equipped to direct such a feature, Whoopi reasoned, "This film really isn't such a departure for Steven, not if you look at his work beyond the obvious special effects. *Close Encounters of the Third Kind* is really about man's search for something more than his everyday life offers him. . . . And I feel like Celie is a lot like [the alien visitor] E.T. [in the Spielberg movie of the same name]. It's a whole new world of discovery for Celie, just as it was for E.T."

The Color Purple, rated PG-13 because of its mature themes, was released in December 1985. The mainstream reviews were mixed. *Time* magazine concluded, "Everyone seems reluctant to let loose here, taking a cue from their too reverent boss." The *New York* magazine reviewer complained, "For over two hours, we look at these tumultuous doings and cardboard characters . . . and we have only the vaguest idea as to how they actually make a living or what their relationships with their neighbors or their community are supposed to be." In contrast, critics such as Roger Ebert of the *Chicago Sun-Times* said, "It is

Oprah Winfrey made her film debut in The Color Purple. (Photofest)

a great, warm, hard, unforgiving, triumphant movie and there is not a scene that does not shine with the love of the people who made it."

Despite arguments surrounding *The Color Purple,* which had been turned out at a cost of $15 million, it grossed $80.26 million in domestic release and made additional revenue overseas. When the Academy Award nominations were announced in February 1986, the film claimed 11 nominations, including Best Picture, Best Actress, and Best Score. However, Spielberg was not nominated as Best Director. Reacting to the obvious snub, Spielberg said with resignation, "When I'm 60, Hollywood will forgive me. I don't know for what, but they'll forgive."

At the Oscar ceremony the next month, *The Color Purple* did not claim a single Academy Award.

Moving On

Deeply disappointed by the uproar that had surrounded *The Color Purple,* Spielberg was undaunted. He continued to produce a large number of feature films (including 1985's *Young Sherlock Holmes* and *Back to the Future,* 1986's *The Money Pit,* 1987's *Inner Space,* and 1988's *Who Framed Roger Rabbit*). His ever-expanding Amblin Entertainment became involved in TV series such as *Amazing Stories* (1985–1987), *Tiny Toon Adventures* (1990–1992), and *The Young Indiana Jones Chronicles* (1992–1993). For the expensively budgeted *Amazing Stories,* a half-hour weekly anthology program, Spielberg directed two episodes and provided the stories for an additional two teleplays. However, the much-promoted *Amazing Stories* was not a hit with home viewers. Observers in the entertainment industry wondered if Steven was not spreading himself too thin, a point of view he came to appreciate better by the early 1990s.

Meanwhile, Steven found a new screenplay he wished to film. It was *Empire of the Sun,* based on a fictionalized autobiography by J. G. Ballard. It concerned a British youth separated from his parents when the Japanese overran Shanghai during World War II. In the narrative, the young man survives a harsh life in a prisoner-of-war camp before eventually being freed by the Allied forces. The movie was to have been directed by the famous British director David Lean, whose feature films—in particular *The Bridge on the River Kwai* and *Lawrence of Arabia*—were standards by which Spielberg always measured himself.

When Lean bowed out of *Empire of the Sun* because of his sudden interest in a different project, Steven took over the reins on this film. It returned Spielberg to a beloved era and subject—World War II. It also dealt with another of the filmmaker's preferred topics: a boy who has a difficult relationship with his dad and finds a father-substitute and an unusual adventure in a strange, unfriendly environment. It addition, it explored the filmmaker's passion for the subject of flying. This theme arises in several of Spielberg's features, although, in real life, he long has had to deal with a fear of such transportation.

Empire of the Sun was shot in England, Spain, and China. Thirteen-year-old Christian Bale from Wales, who had appeared with Spielberg's wife Amy in a 1986 TV movie, was cast in the main role. It was an extremely demanding assignment for young Bale to interpret the once-spoiled Jim Graham, who undergoes horrific conditions in the prisoner camp and, in the process, gains a new outlook on life.

Many reviewers were impressed by the film's strong visuals and admired the first half of the picture. In con-

Christian Bale, Spielberg, and John Malkovich (left to right) on the set of Empire of the Sun *(1987). Although the film earned several Academy Award nominations, it was not a commercial success.* (Photofest)

trast, they were far less enchanted as *Empire of the Sun* dragged on to its conclusion. Perhaps best summing up the critics' (and filmgoers') confusion on Spielberg's overall aim here, Pauline Kael (*New Yorker*) wrote, "You come out saying, 'What was that about?' "

Empire of the Sun yielded six Academy Award nominations (in such categories as Best Cinematography and Best Editing), but none, as expected, for Spielberg's contributions. Made at a cost of $38 million, the 154-minute entry was a financial disappointment, gathering only $66.7 million in its global distribution. Said Spielberg, who knew from the start that the film's subject matter was not geared for mass audiences, "I've earned the right to fail commercially."

Indy to the Rescue

Accepting temporarily that the public preferred his "popcorn movies," Spielberg retreated to the safety of the *Indiana Jones* screen franchise. He agreed to make a third entry in the adventure series with George Lucas. Doing so meant that he had to forgo directing *Rain Man*, a project to which he'd already devoted several months' work.

Having learned from *Indiana Jones and the Temple of Doom* that audiences did not expect nor appreciate too much graphic violence, Spielberg and Lucas toned down the action in this follow-up. This time the film's opening—set in 1912—focused on the hero as a young man. With actor River Phoenix playing the young Indiana Jones, this sequence established a fitting nostalgic tone for the rest of the movie. In an example of smart casting, Sean Connery played the archeologist father of Indiana Jones, who was once again portrayed by Harrison Ford. A definite "Spielbergian" touch was having Connery and Ford engage in a battle of the generations, as father and son compete for authority and even vie for the attention of beautiful female characters.

Considered by all to be an improvement over the second installment, *Indiana Jones and the Last Crusade*, made at a cost of $48 million, enjoyed a worldwide gross of $495 million. Pleased that he had won back his mass appeal, Spielberg thought this third chapter in the Indy saga would end his association with the character. He said jokingly, "I feel as if I have graduated from the college of Cliffhanger U." However, before long he was drawn back into the fray with a video game based on the series, and was then selected to help produce a series of TV movies *Young Indiana Jones Chronicles* in 1992 to 1993. Finally, more than a decade later, Steven prepared for a fourth installment of the Indiana Jones movie series.

Always and Beyond

As a youngster growing up in Phoenix, Arizona, Steven had enjoyed watching the 1943 television film *A Guy Named Joe*. This romantic fable, dealing with bravery and loss during World War II, produced a strong emotional response in Spielberg. He would call the glossy MGM feature, costarring Spencer Tracy, Irene Dunne, and Van Johnson, a "story that touched my soul" and "the second movie after *Bambi* that made me cry." Since 1980 Steven had been hoping to remake it, but other projects kept taking priority.

Finally, in 1988, Spielberg began the venture, now called *Always*, in earnest. Fearing that contemporary audiences would not respond properly to a dreamy tale set in the wartime 1940s, he updated the action to the present and relocated the setting from an island military base in the Pacific Ocean to Montana, where the central characters are involved in firefighting. When the key character, a cocky pilot (played by Richard Dreyfuss) dies on duty, the aviator regrets never having expressed his love for a copilot and radio dispatcher (Holly Hunter). With the help of an angel (Audrey Hepburn) Dreyfuss returns to Earth as a ghostly presence. He gives job advice to his replacement (Brad Johnson), a handsome young man who soon falls in love with the mourning Hunter. By the finale, the deceased hero comes to terms with his earthly loss and moves on spiritually so the couple on Earth can find happiness together.

Once again tackling a mature emotional theme, Spielberg faced the difficult task of making audiences respond to a brash Dreyfuss as the eventually helpful, unseen spirit. While moviegoers appreciated the movie's striking visuals—especially the forest fire sequences—they generally did not care about the filmmaker's dated fantasy or the often-immature approach to the complex emotions shown on camera. Created at a cost of $29.5 million, the unsatisfying *Always*, made for Universal/United Artists release, grossed only $43.8 million in domestic distribution.

Actress Amy Irving and Spielberg separated in 1989 after almost four years of marriage. (Photofest)

Many people thought Spielberg chose to make *Always* to cope with an emotional loss he was experiencing during this period. With the workaholic Steven so often away from home (especially during the difficult location shoot for *Indiana Jones and the Last Crusade*), Amy Irving felt continually abandoned by her spouse. A dedicated and ambitious actress, she came to believe that being married to Spielberg was damaging her acting career. She reasoned that other directors feared or refused to hire her because she was his wife. On the other hand, being wed to the film mogul had not earned her much work from Steven's Amblin Entertainment. (She had been a singing voice in their animated feature entry, *Who Framed Roger Rabbit*.) Amy also wanted a simpler lifestyle than the wife of Hollywood's most famous director allowed. Thus, their pending divorce was announced in April 1989 with the couple agreeing to share custody of their son Max. Just as he had been emotionally torn apart by his parents' divorce years earlier, so Steven was thrown off course by his own broken marriage.

Although Steven's life had hit a downward creative and emotional spiral as the 1980s ended, the trend would soon change.

6

TO NEVERLAND AND BACK

Although Steven Spielberg's life had hit a downward creative and emotional spiral as the 1980s ended, the trend would soon change. In the 1990s Steven would discover newfound domestic happiness and an upswing in his career path—including some of the professional awards he had coveted for so long.

A New Beginning

After Steven Spielberg and Amy Irving divorced in 1989, the filmmaker renewed his romantic relationship with actress Kate Capshaw, the leading lady of *Indiana Jones and the Temple of Doom*. She gave birth to their child, a daughter named Sasha, in May 1990. Following Kate's conversion to Judaism, the couple wed in October 1991 at

Spielberg with wife Kate Capshaw. (Photofest)

their country home in East Hampton, Long Island, New York. Their growing family unit not only included Sasha, but Steven's son Max by Amy Irving and Kate's daughter Jessica by a previous marriage. In addition, there was

Theo, a foster child the newlyweds adopted. Three more children—Sawyer, Destry, and Mikaela, whom the couple adopted—followed over the next five years.

Revisiting a Childhood Favorite

Now a contented family man, Spielberg still retained that inner child so long a key part of his personality. As if to put that aspect of him to rest as he entered middle age, he finally made a movie about one of his favorite childhood characters and stories: Peter Pan. Rather than simply remake Sir James Barrie's famous play, which had been filmed several times before (including Walt Disney's animated feature), Steven had more ambitious plans. He wanted to explore the theme of what might have happened if had Peter Pan grown up into a work-obsessed family man and if the dastardly pirate Captain Hook had not died.

Assuming that Spielberg would bring his golden touch to the Peter Pan project—now called *Hook*—TriStar Pictures gave Steven a big budget to make this fantasy adventure. As it shaped up, the elaborate production was to feature Robin Williams as the adult, workaholic Peter Pan, Dustin Hoffman as the swaggering buccaneer villain, and, in a guest role, Julia Roberts as the magical pixie Tinkerbell. Production began at London soundstage facilities in 1991 and ran nearly six weeks over its already lengthy 76-day shooting schedule. Thereafter, the picture's complicated special effects added in postproduction proved far more difficult to achieve than had been anticipated. Originally budgeted at $48 million, the film's costs soared to $70 million. When finally released in December 1991, the feature met with rather negative reviews. The entertainment trade paper *Daily Variety* complained, "*Hook* feels as much like a massive amusement park ride as it does a film. . . . A shade sophisticated for small kids and too indulgent for more demanding adults."

Putting the *Hook* experience into perspective, Spielberg recognized that he had been "seduced by my own success. I had always played to the adult audience who were able to remember their childhood and enjoy the movies along with their own children, but when I began playing to the kids directly, I found that I stumbled on my shoelaces." Steven realized that, "When you're making movies, you can't do things consciously."

Thundering Dinosaurs

Back in the late 1960s when Spielberg had first joined Universal Studios as a director, he had met Michael Crichton, then visiting the film facility. Over subsequent years, Steven and the doctor-turned-novelist stayed in touch. By the late 1980s, Crichton had written a screenplay about his hectic years in the emergency room of a major

Boston hospital. He sought Spielberg's advice in getting the project produced. Eventually, the property became the hit NBC-TV series *ER*, of which Spielberg's Amblin Entertainment was a producer. Meanwhile, Michael discussed with Steven an exciting novel he had written and which was about to be published. *Jurassic Park* deals with a billionaire scientist who perfects the cloning of supposedly long-extinct dinosaurs, which he employs as the main attraction of a huge theme park he has built on an island. The reptiles—of both flesh-chomping and plant-eating varieties—break free from captivity and threaten to kill all those on the isle, including several children.

Steven envisioned *Jurassic Park* as a sequel, on land, to his past mega-hit, *Jaws*. At the end of a huge bidding war in 1990, Spielberg and Universal Pictures won the screen rights to Crichton's book. Over the next two years, the filmmaker and his large staff mapped out the intricate project with detailed storyboards. Spielberg was determined that this time, unlike with *Hook* or *1941*, the production would not get out of financial control.

By now, movie audiences demanded much more sophistication in the presentation of monsters than had been acceptable even 15 years earlier with Spielberg's own *Jaws*. Thus, the old stop-motion technique of moving a miniature after exposing each film frame or two would no longer suffice. As such, Steven first considered using robotic dinosaurs to populate *Jurassic Park*. However, he quickly realized that such mechanical reptiles would not produce the desired effect of giving these mammoth creatures "real" personality. Next, he turned to animatronics (the use of electronics to animate puppets or other created figures) as a mean of bringing his massive dinosaurs to "life." As time progressed, the filmmaker explored more sophisticated technical means. He now envisioned using both Go-Motion (a motor-controlled, computerized system to operate movements of miniature models as film frames are exposed) in addition to computer-generated imagery (CGI) effects.

Visual effects supervisor Dennis Muren told Spielberg that with recent advances in computer technology and software he was sure his department could produce full-scale dinosaurs with computer graphics. While Muren and his squad set about proving their boast, Steven found himself learning sophisticated aspects of computer technology. Several of these principles were based on the type of research that Steven's father, Arnold, a pioneer in the computer field, had been investigating over past decades. When the filmmaker saw the impressive results of Muren's tests, he realized that the newly improved CGI effects were the *only* way to go. Thus Spielberg relied on this ever-advancing technology for creating some of the lifelike giant creatures that filled *Jurassic Park*.

Directing a dinosaur on the set of Jurassic Park *(1993).* (Photofest)

Production got underway in Hawaii (which substituted for the film's locale off the coast of Costa Rica) in August 1992. The shooting wrapped in Hollywood at the end of that November—ahead of schedule. The thriller debuted in June 1993. Filled with both a sense of wonder and tremendous fear of these colossal creatures, *Jurassic Park* was a wild, entertaining ride for filmgoers as they watched the tyrannosaurus rex, velociraptors, triceratops, and others from the distant past run amok on the tropical island.

Made for $63 million, *Jurassic Park* achieved a worldwide box-office gross of more than $913 million, making it the most profitable film in the history of the movies to that date. The film won three Academy Awards, including Oscars for Best Visual Effects and Best Sound. So enthusiastic was the public's reaction to this massive hit that it prompted video games, a slew of other merchandizing tie-ins, and the inevitable film sequels. By the time that Spielberg readied *The Lost World: Jurassic Park* (1997), based on another Michael Crichton best-seller, CGI technology had advanced so far that reliance on remote control mechanical puppets and other animated means could be relegated to the past. That impressive sequel, budgeted at $73 million, drew in $239 million at the domestic box office. For *Jurassic Park III* (2001), executive producer Spielberg turned over the director's reins to Joe Johnston. The third installment grossed $181 million in domestic box-office sales, based on a $93 million budget.

Rediscovering His Jewish Roots

When Thomas Keneally's book *Schindler's List* was published in 1982, Spielberg was immediately drawn to its spellbinding story of the crafty industrialist and staunch member of the Czechoslovakian Nazi Party who saved over 1,100 Jews from death in German concentration camps. The well-received book detailed how devil-may-care Schindler, who had begun protecting his Jewish workers as a way to gain cheap labor, underwent a dramatic change of heart. Schindler became motivated by a sense of humanity to save as many as possible of "his" persecuted flock from extinction. In the process, Schindler risked not only his fortune but also his life.

At the time Spielberg was unsure if he should direct the wrenching drama, fearing he was not really ready to tackle such strong subject matter. Nevertheless, Universal Pictures acquired the film rights to *Schindler's List*, hoping that Steven would one day change his mind about translating this important story to the screen. As the years passed, Spielberg could not decide whether or not to lead this Holocaust-themed drama. At one point, he tried to convince Polish-born filmmaker Roman Polanski, a victim of the Nazis, to direct the project. However, Polanski did not want to revisit such painful memories at that time.

By 1990, Spielberg was becoming more convinced that he must direct *Schindler's List*. He was helped in his decision when his bride-to-be, Kate Capshaw, converted to Judaism. While sharing in her study of the Jewish faith, he experienced a yearning to explore more fully his own religious roots. It was a feeling that had been growing within him since the birth of his first child, Max, in 1985. Two years later Steven felt emotionally ready to make the somber *Schindler's List*. He understood that undertaking this film would force him to deal with his repressed feelings about having experienced anti-Semitism as a youth.

Once he'd made his commitment to move ahead with the film, Spielberg passed up directing the 1992 remake of *Cape Fear*, which was being produced by his Amblin

Entertainment. As a prerequisite of Universal studio's financing the $25 million for *Schindler's List*, Spielberg agreed to finish work on *Jurassic Park* first.

Once his dinosaur epic was complete, Spielberg started preproduction on *Schindler's List*. By now he greatly identified with Oskar Schindler a (lapsed) Catholic who sacrificed great material success to undertake a heartfelt challenge. To play the gentile "hero," a man of contradictory emotions and often-unexplainable motives, he cast Irish actor Liam Neeson. Ben Kingsley (the Oscar-winning star of *Gandhi*) was signed to be Itzhak Stern, a Jewish accountant who wisely guides Schindler through his dangerous acts of bravery on behalf of fellow Holocaust victims. Rounding out the trio of lead roles in *Schindler's List* was Ralph Fiennes. He appears as the sadistic Nazi officer in charge of the local concentration camp.

Insisting on shooting this saga where it had taken place more than 50 years earlier, Spielberg scouted locations in Krakow, Poland, including the remnants of the old Jewish ghetto, as well as the sites of Schindler's apartment and enamelware factory. Authorities from the World Jewish Congress, concerned that the popular moviemaker would make the story too "Hollywood," refused permission for Steven to film inside Auschwitz (one of the largest and most notorious of the Nazi concentrations camps during World War II). As a result, Spielberg had a replica constructed near its actual locale in southern Poland.

Liam Neeson (right), as Oskar Schindler, receives direction from Spielberg on the set of Schindler's List *(1993).* (Literature/Film Archive)

The largely black-and-white filming began in March 1993 in bitter cold weather, with Steven guiding a cast of 124, as many as 3,000 extras, and a crew of over 200, through 35 locations and nearly 148 different sets. Particularly in supervising the recreation of the razing of the Jewish ghetto in Krakow and the murdering of its remaining inhabitants, a deeply moved Spielberg said, "I feel like more of a journalist than a director on this movie. . . . I recreated these events, and then I experienced them as any witness or victim would have. It wasn't like a movie." Steven was so stirred by these experiences, that he would often leave the set at night emotionally drained and in tears.

Working from his heart, Spielberg completed the three-month shoot that spring. For this effort he largely abandoned his usual flashy filmmaking style. As he explained in a *Harper's Bazaar* interview: "On this movie I threw out the toolbox and started from scratch. I think I got rid of some of what I do to make a movie kind of slick . . . everything that for me might be considered a safety net." He also noted, "I would have ruined it had I made this 10 years ago."

Released in December 1993, *Schindler's List* was dedicated to the "memory of the more than 6 million Jews murdered." Writing in the *New York Times*, Janet Maslin judged, "Rising brilliantly to the challenge of this material and displaying an electrifying creative intelligence, Mr. Spielberg has made sure that neither he nor the Holocaust will ever be thought of in the same way again. With every frame, he demonstrates the power of the filmmaker to distill complex events into fiercely indelible images."

Schindler's List was nominated for 12 Academy Awards. It won seven, including one for Spielberg as Best Director. In accepting his long-desired Oscar, Steven humbly acknowledged the many millions of victims of World War II. He also expressed his hope that this movie would counteract the trend in recent years among some Americans to

Spielberg helps high school students with a CD-ROM of Holocaust-survivor testimonies. This is part of his effort, on behalf of the Shoah Foundation, to bring survivors' stories to life through audio and video. (Associated Press, Shoah Foundation)

sweep the Holocaust under the carpet as if the shocking horrors had never happened.

New Directions

In 1994, Spielberg realized a longtime dream of founding his own Los Angeles-based film studio. Joined by former Disney Studio top executive Jeffrey Katzenberg and record industry mogul David Geffen, Steven formed DreamWorks SKG. It was a hugely ambitious undertaking that required tremendous financial funding (which came from both the primary partners and outside investors). Its first feature film release would be 1997's *The Peacemaker*, an action yarn directed by Mimi Leder, and costarring George Clooney and Nicole Kidman.

Now, as he approached age 50, Steven thought increasingly of giving back to the world some of the bounty he had received over the years. While he had been a frequent charity donor over recent decades, he wanted to do something special and particularly meaningful to him. Thus, with his profits from *Schindler's List,* he founded the Survivors of the Shoah Visual History Foundation. ("Shoah" is the Hebrew word for the Holocaust.) The organization's ambition was to "create an audiovisual archive of firsthand testimonies." In the next years, the Foundation recorded the personal testimonies of more than 50,000 survivors of World War II horrors.

Through DreamWorks, Spielberg continued to produce a wide range of movie products of varying quality and genres, including *Casper* (1995), *High Incident* (1996; TV series), *Twister* (1996), *Men in Black* (1997), and *The Mask of Zorro* (1998). After a four-year breather, Steven returned to directing "popcorn films" with 1997's *The Lost World: Jurassic Park*. That same year, he produced and directed

Jeffrey Katzenberg, Steven Spielberg, and David Geffen (left to right) announce the creation of DreamWorks SKG. (Associated Press)

Amistad, which deals with the 1839 bloody mutiny aboard a Spanish slave ship off the coast of Cuba. The African mutineers are later captured and taken to New Haven, Connecticut, where they are placed on trial. A good deal of the narrative involves the courtroom drama surrounding the slave (played by Djimon Hounsou) who led the revolt. Made with earnest intent, the R-rated (for violence) movie amounted to what many called a much too long (152 minutes), often static history lesson. It won only a modest response from filmgoers and critics.

Back to World War II

Returning to a favored topic—World War II—Spielberg produced and directed *Saving Private Ryan* in 1998. Unlike the buffoonery of his *1941*, this was a somber study of warfare and combat's many effects on troops. For inspiration, Spielberg watched several documentaries about World War II, and viewed such classic combat features as William Wellman's *The Story of G. I. Joe* (1945) and *Battleground* (1949), Samuel Fuller's *The Steel Helmet* (1951), and Don Siegel's *Hell Is for Heroes* (1962).

The American squad at the center of *Saving Private Ryan* is under the command of Captain John Miller, played by Tom Hanks. Their task is to pass through heavily fortified German military positions in France in order to reach the front lines of battle and rescue a U.S. soldier (played by Matt Damon) whose three brothers were killed in military action in the same week. Captain Miller's orders are to save the soldier so that he may be returned home to his family. In the course of rescuing Damon, most of the detachment is killed. The finale flashes ahead to the present in which an elderly G.I. visits graves of those killed in action.

Saving Private Ryan has become famous for its opening 20-minute segment. It re-created the bloody D-Day assault in June 1944 as Allied troops stormed the Germans forces at Omaha Beach in France. Never was Steven more masterful as a filmmaker than in this highly charged extended

Spielberg revisited the theme of World War II in his Academy Award winning film Saving Private Ryan *(1999).* (Photofest)

sequence, filled with gore and the explosive sounds of death. Filmed by Janusz Kaminski (who had been the cinematographer on several Spielberg pictures including *Schindler's List* and *Amistad*), the footage is among the most graphic of any war film. Made for $70 million, the feature grossed $216 million in domestic distribution with a similar amount earned from ticket admissions overseas.

At the Oscar ceremonies in March 1999, *Saving Private Ryan*, nominated for 11 Academy Awards, won several trophies. Among the five Oscars it claimed was another Best Director award for Spielberg and an award for camerawork for Kaminski. Accepting his latest prize as Best Director, Spielberg acknowledged "the families who lost sons in World War II." Then, in tribute to his own father who had served on battlefields in the 1940s, Steven said, "Dad, you're the greatest. Thank you for showing me that there is honor in looking back and respecting the past. I love you very much. This is for you."

Moving into the Future

When acclaimed filmmaker Stanley Kubrick died in March 1999, he was in preproduction on a science-fiction movie, *A.I. Artificial Intelligence*. His friend Spielberg was asked to take over the complex cinema project. Steven accepted the challenge, putting aside thoughts of filming a biography of aviator Charles Lindbergh or making a screen adaptation of the novel, *Memoirs of a Geisha*. Spielberg was excited by the idea of bringing Kubrick's vision to reality.

A.I. was based on a short story ("Super Toys Last All Summer Long") by Brian Aldiss. It deals with a time in the near future where scientists have developed a sophisticated (ultimate) robot that can experience a range of emotions, including love. Spielberg, in writing his first full script since *Close Encounters of the Third Kind*, restructured the narrative to focus on favored themes—especially that of the Pinocchio tale in which a puppet desperately wishes to become a real boy. Here the juvenile character is a robot boy (played by Haley Joel Osment) who is adopted by a devoted couple who has lost their son and is seeking an emotional replacement.

Boasting fine cinematography from Janusz Kaminski, production design by Rick Carter, and a score by another longtime Spielberg associate, John Williams, *A.I.* ultimately proved to be an unsatisfying filmgoing experience for many viewers. As critic Roger Ebert (*Chicago Sun-Times*) said of the June 2001 release, "Here is one of the most ambitious films of recent years, filled with wondrous sights and provocative ideas, but it miscalculates in asking us to invest our emotions in a character that is, after all, a machine." Made on a hefty $90 million, the picture—a hybrid of Spielberg and Kubrick concepts—grossed $78.6 million at the domestic box-office, with another $39.1 million grossed from European distribution.

Not slackening his professional pace, Spielberg kept busy producing television projects, including *Band of Brothers* (2001), an ambitious made-for-cable miniseries about a U.S. Army Paratrooper division and their harrowing World War II mission in France. The much-lauded, 10-part drama utilized eight directors, including Tom Hanks. *Taken* (2002), a 20-hour drama for the Sci-Fi Channel, relied on 10 directors (including Tobe Hooper of *Poltergeist*) to present a story that spans five decades. It revolves around four generations of a trio of families involved in abductions by aliens and how one such byproduct of alien interference (played by Dakota Fanning) holds the answer to civilization's future.

Continuing in a futuristic mode, Steven next directed *Minority Report* (2002), a lavish sci-fi thriller based on a Philip K. Dick short story. Set in 2054, it revolves around a U.S. government agency scheme to prevent crimes *before* they happen—using three psychics, who, with the assistance of an intricate computer system, help department agents visualize homicides before they occur. Made on a massive $102 million budget to encompass a slick physical vision of a futuristic landscape, *Minority Report* was a further extension of the growing pessimism that now filtered through Spielberg's storytelling. Kenneth Turan (*Los Angeles Times*) wrote, "It took paranoid visionary Philip K. Dick to do what Stanley Kubrick [in *A.I. Artificial Intelligence*] could not: Get Steven Spielberg to fully cross over to the dark side. The question now is, how happy are we to have him there?" The same reviewer observed, "This is a film that gives us a lot to chew on, but not all of it has been properly digested."

Rebounding

In December 2002, seven months after *Minority Report* opened to less than sensational critical and audience response, came Spielberg's next film: *Catch Me If You Can*. It was based on a true-life case and was shot quickly (two months) and efficiently ($52 million). This lighthearted account concerns a charming young con artist (played by Leonardo DiCaprio) who adopts a series of disguises, including that of a physician, assistant attorney general, airline pilot, and teacher. In his different guises, he travels around the world cashing millions of dollars in fraudulent checks. An FBI agent (played by Tom Hanks) pursues and eventually captures the young con man. The culprit is sent to prison, but a twist of fate provides an ironic future for the lawbreaker.

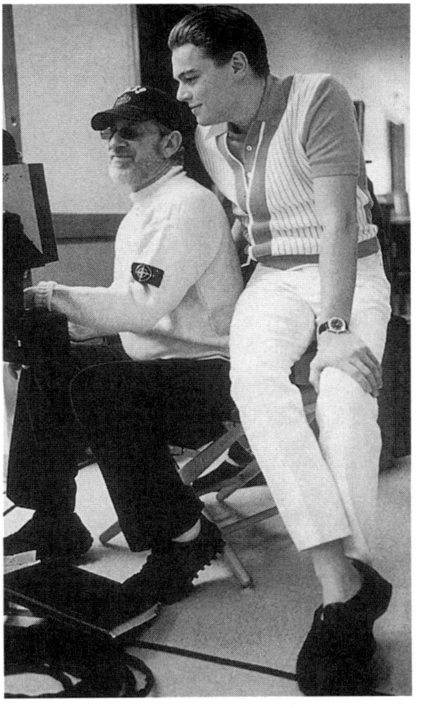

Spielberg and Leonardo DiCaprio on the set of Catch Me If You Can *(2002).* (Photofest)

Mick LaSalle (*San Francisco Examiner*) described *Catch Me If You Can*: "It may have moments of seriousness that are effective, and relationships that are presented with depth and sincerity that add to our enjoyment. But what lingers in the memory is the impression of having experienced a frolic, a ride through the park on a bright winter day." Even in this whimsical film, several recurrent Spielberg themes emerged: a broken marriage, the son trying to piece the union back together, and the young central character dealing with an unsettling relationship with his father. As in several of Spielberg's earlier screen works, Steven utilizes a happy ending to wrap up the movie. The film met with many favorable reviews.

Looking Ahead

As Spielberg's career moves further into the 21st century, he continues to maintain his high rank and tremendous power in Hollywood, where he is known as a tough dealmaker. Whether mentoring young filmmakers (including son Max), creating new video games and CD-ROM educational discs, or supervising DVD sets of his past cinematic achievements, Steven keeps a firm hold on moviegoers' interest. He also continues to receive new honors for his impressive body of screen work. In 2001 he was made an honorary knight of the British Empire because his career "has had a global impact." In May 2002 Steven received an honorary degree from Yale University for his "artistry and imagination" in his movies which "entertain, engage, and enlighten." In that same month he also graduated from

Sitting among his fellow California State University, Long Beach graduates in May 2002, Steven Spielberg completes the college degree he began in 1965. (Associated Press)

California State University, Long Beach, having completed the degree program he began almost 40 years earlier.

Looking to the future, Spielberg understands the difficulty of outdoing his past professional achievements. However, he believes, "Every movie I make is a new challenge. I'll have big hit movies and I'll have films that aren't big hits, and that's just what happens when you're a filmmaker and you're putting your things out there for the public."

Having risen so successfully through the ranks of the movie industry, Steven's advice to aspiring filmmakers is, "Start as young as you possibly can and make your own films, rather than reading about people who have made their own film. There is no substitute for getting out there and shooting, cutting, and then showing—especially showing, especially listening to the audience and seeing how tuned in you are to their need." As to achieving success in this highly competitive profession, Spielberg says, "A lot of it is luck, and a lot of it is wanting it so much that you're going to take the hinges off the door to get it open."

TIME LINE

1946 Steven Spielberg born in Cincinnati, Ohio, on December 18, the first of four children

1949 Moves with family to Camden, New Jersey

1957 Directs first amateur film, the eight-millimeter short, *The Last Train Wreck*; family moves to suburb of Phoenix, Arizona

1958 Directs *The Last Gunfight*, one of several increasingly more intricate amateur shorts

1962 His 40-minute combat picture, *Escape to Nowhere*, wins a statewide filmmaking competition.

1964 Directs *Firelight*, a 140-minute science-fiction-themed feature that premieres in Phoenix; Spielbergs relocate to northern California, ultimately living in Saratoga

1965 Enters Long Beach State College in southern California

1968 Produces and directs the 35-millimeter short, *Amblin'*, which wins a prize at the Atlanta Film Festival in 1969

1969 Offered a seven-year directing contract at Universal Studios, leaves college; makes his professional debut directing Joan Crawford in the "Eyes" episode of the TV movie *Night Gallery*

1971 Directs the made-for-TV movie *Duel,* which receives critical acclaim; in 1974 the film is expanded for theatrical release abroad

1974 *The Sugarland Express* is released by Universal.

1975 *Jaws* (Universal) becomes a box-office bonanza.

1977 *Close Encounters of the Third Kind* (Columbia) debuts in the fall, leading to his first Academy Award nomination as Best Director; revised special edition of *Close Encounters* issued in 1979

1979 *1941* (Universal/Columbia) opens.

1981 *Raiders of the Lost Ark* (Paramount) debuts, made in conjunction with producer and director friend George Lucas.

1982 *E.T. the Extra-Terrestrial* is released by Universal; *Poltergeist* (Paramount), written and produced by Spielberg and directed by Tobe Hooper, opens.

1984 *Indiana Jones and the Temple of Doom* is distributed by Paramount; forms Amblin Entertainment and continues to produce other directors' features

1985 *The Color Purple* (Warner Bros.) opens; enters into a deal with NBC-TV to produce and occasionally direct the *Amazing Stories* series; son Max born to actress Amy Irving, whom he weds later in the year

1987 *Empire of the Sun* (Warner Bros.) premieres; the filmmaker earns a special Academy Award for "creative production."

1989 *Indiana Jones and the Last Crusade* (Paramount) and *Always* (Universal/United Artists) premiere; divorces Irving

1990 Birth of daughter Sasha; weds actress Kate Capshaw; adopts foster child Theo

1991 *Hook* (TriStar) is released.

1992 Birth of son Sawyer

1993 *Jurassic Park* and *Schindler's List* open; receives Oscar for Best Director and Best Picture for *Schindler's List*

1994 Forms a new studio (DreamWorks SKG) with Jeffrey Katzenberg and David Geffen; establishes Survivors of the Shoal Visual History Foundation

1996 Birth of daughter Destry; adopts Mikaela

1997 *The Lost World: Jurassic Park* (Universal) and *Amistad* (DreamWorks) are released.

1998 *Saving Private Ryan* (DreamWorks/Paramount) opens; earns Oscar for Best Director

2001 *A.I.: Artificial Intelligence* (Warner Bros.) opens; produces the HBO cable TV miniseries *Band of Brothers*

2002 *Minority Report* (Twentieth Century-Fox) and *Catch Me If You Can* (DreamWorks) premiere; produces the Sci-Fi Channel TV miniseries *Taken*

2003 Begins preproduction on the fourth *Indiana Jones* screen installment, *Terminal*, and *The Secret Life of Walter Mitty*

HOW TO BECOME A FILMMAKER

THE JOB

Film directors, also called *filmmakers,* are considered to bear ultimate responsibility for the tone and quality of the films they work on. They interpret the stories and narratives presented in scripts and coordinate the filming of their interpretations. They are involved in preproduction, production, and postproduction. They audition, select, and rehearse the acting crew. They work on matters regarding set designs, musical scores, and costumes; and they decide on details such as where scenes should be shot, what backgrounds might be needed, and how special effects could be employed.

The director of a film often works with a *casting director,* who is in charge of auditioning performers. The casting director pays close attention to attributes of the performers such as physical appearance, quality of voice, and acting ability and experience, and then presents to the director a list of suitable candidates for each role.

One of the most important aspects of the film director's job is working with the performers. Directors have their own styles of extracting accurate emotion and performance from cast members, but they must be dedicated to this goal.

Two common techniques that categorize directors' styles are montage and mise-en-scène. *Montage directors* are concerned with using editing techniques to produce desired results; they consider it important to focus on how individual shots will work when pieced together with others. Consider Alfred Hitchcock (1899–1980), who directed the production of one scene in *Psycho,* for example, by filming discrete shots in a bathroom and then editing in dialogue, sound effects, and music to create tremendous suspense. *Mise-en-scène directors* are more concerned with the pre-editing phase, focusing on the elements of angles, movement, and design one shot at a time, as Orson Welles (1915–85) did. Many directors combine elements of both techniques in their work.

The film's *art director* creates set-design concepts and chooses shoot locations. He or she meets with the filmmaker and producer to set budgets and schedules, and then accordingly coordinates the construction of sets. Research is done on the period in which the film is to take place, and experts are consulted to help create appropriate architectural and environmental styles. The art director also is often involved in design ideas for costumes, makeup and hairstyles, photographic effects, and other elements of the film's production.

The *director of photography,* or *cinematographer,* is responsible for organizing and implementing the actual camera work. Together with the filmmaker, he or she interprets scenes and decides on appropriate camera motion to achieve desired results. The director of photography determines the amounts of natural and artificial lighting required for each shoot, as well as such technical factors as the type of film to be used, camera angles and distance, depth of field, and focus.

Motion pictures are usually filmed out of sequence, meaning that the ending might be shot first and scenes from the middle of the story might not be filmed until the end of production. Directors are responsible for scheduling each day's sequence of scenes; they coordinate filming so that scenes using the same set and performers will be filmed together. In addition to conferring with the art director and the director of photography, filmmakers meet with technicians and crew members to advise on and approve final scenery, lighting, props, and other necessary equipment. They are also involved with final approval of costumes, choreography, and music.

After all the scenes have been shot, postproduction begins. The director works with picture and sound editors to cut apart and piece together the final reels. The *film editor* shares the director's vision about the picture and assembles shots according to that overall idea, synchronizing film with voice and sound tracks produced by the *sound editor* and *music editor.*

While the director supervises all major aspects of film production, various assistants help throughout the process. In a less creative position than the filmmaker's, the *first assistant director* organizes various practical matters involved during the shooting of each scene. The *second assistant director* is a coordinator who works as a liaison among the production office, the first assistant director, and the performers. The *second unit director* coordinates sequences such as scenic inserts and action shots that do not involve the main acting crew.

REQUIREMENTS

High School

Film and television directors' careers are rather nontraditional. There is no standard training outline involved, no normal progression up a movie industry ladder leading to the director's job. At the very least, a high school diploma, while not technically required if you wish to become a director, will still probably be indispensable to you in terms of the background and education it signifies. As is true of all artists, especially those in a medium as widely disseminated as film, you will need to have rich and varied experiences in order to create works that are intelligently crafted and speak to people of many different backgrounds. In high school, courses in English, art, theater, and history will give you a good foundation. Further, a high school diploma will be necessary if you decide to go on to film school. Be active in school and community drama productions, whether as a performer, set designer, or cue-card holder.

Postsecondary Training

In college and afterward, take film classes and volunteer to work on other students' films. Dedication, talent, and experience have always been indispensable to a director. No doubt it is beneficial to become aware of one's passion for film as early as possible. Woody Allen, for example, recognized early in his life the importance motion pictures held for him, but he worked as a magician, jazz clarinet player, joke writer, and stand-up comic before ever directing films. Allen took few film courses in his life.

On the other hand, many successful directors such as Francis Ford Coppola and Martha Coolidge have taken the formal film school route. There are more than 500 film studies programs offered by schools of higher education throughout the United States, including those considered to be the five most reputable: the American Film Institute in Los Angeles, Columbia University in New York City, New York University, the University of California at Los Angeles (UCLA), and the University of Southern California. These schools have film professionals on their faculties and provide a very visible stage for student talent, as they are all located in the two film-business hot spots, California and New York. (The tuition for film programs offered elsewhere, however, tends to be much less expensive than at these schools.)

Film school offers overall formal training, and provides an education in fundamental directing skills by working with student productions. Such education is rigorous, but in addition to teaching skills it provides aspiring directors with peer groups and a network of contacts with students, faculty, and guest speakers that can be of help after graduation.

The debate continues on what is more influential in a directing career: film school or personal experience. Some say that it is possible for creative people to land directing jobs without having gone through a formal program. Competition is so pervasive in the industry that even film school graduates find jobs scarce (only 5 to 10 percent of the 26,000 students who graduate from film schools each year find jobs in the industry). Martha Coolidge, for instance, made independent films for 10 years before directing a Hollywood movie.

Other Requirements

Konstantin Stanislavsky had a passion for his directorial work in the theater, believing that it was an art of immense social importance. Today's motion picture directors must have similar inspiration and possibly even greater creative strength, because of the additional responsibilities involved in directing modern film.

EXPLORING

If you are a would-be director, the most obvious opportunity for exploration lies in your own imagination. Being drawn to films and captivated by the process of how they are made is the beginning of the filmmaker's journey.

In high school and beyond, those interested in becoming directors should pay attention to motion pictures. Watch them at every opportunity, both at the theater and at home. Study your favorite television shows to see what makes them interesting. Two major trade publications to read are *Variety* (www.variety.com) and *Hollywood Reporter* (www.hollywoodreporter.com). The Directors Guild of America's official publication *DGA Magazine* contains much information on the industry. If you are unable to find this magazine at a public library or bookstore, visit the DGA website (www.dga.org) to read sample articles. Also, the book *How to Make It in Hollywood: All the Right Moves* (Linda Buzzell, 1996, Harper Perennial) is a very good informal guide that presents insider tips on such factors as "schmoozing" and chutzpah (self-confidence) as well as an extensive list of valuable resources.

During summers, many camps and workshops offer programs for high school students interested in film work. For example, UCLA presents its Media Workshops for students ages 14 to 24. Classes focus on mass media production, including film, TV, and video. For information, contact the Media Workshops Foundation, Tel.: 1-800-223-4561, Web: www.mediaworkshops.org/foundation.

EMPLOYERS

Employment as a film or television director is usually on a freelance or contractual basis. Directors find work, for example, with film studios (both major and independent), at television stations and cable networks, through advertising agencies, with record companies, and through the creation of their own independent film projects.

STARTING OUT

It is considered difficult to begin as a motion picture director. With nontraditional steps to professional status, the occupation poses challenges for those seeking employment. However, there is some solid advice for those who wish to direct motion pictures.

Many current directors began their careers in other film industry professions, such as acting or writing. Consider Jodie Foster, who appeared in 30 films and dozens of television productions before she went on to direct her first motion picture at the age of 28. Obviously it helps to grow up near the heart of "Tinseltown" (Hollywood) and to have the influence of one's family spurring you on. The support of family and friends is often cited as an essential element in shaping the confidence you need to succeed in the industry.

As mentioned earlier, film school is a breeding ground for making contacts. Often, contacts are the essential factor in getting a job; many Hollywood insiders agree that it's not what you know, but who you know that will get you in. Networking often leads to good opportunities at various types of jobs in the industry. Many professionals recommend that those who want to become directors should go to Los Angeles or New York, find any industry-related job, continue to take classes, and keep their eyes and ears open for news of job openings, especially with those professionals who are admired for their talent.

One program to be aware of is the Assistant Directors Training Program of the Directors Guild of America. This program provides an excellent opportunity for those without industry connections to work on film and television productions. The program is based in two locations, New York City for the East Coast Program and Sherman Oaks, California, for the West Coast Program. Trainees receive hands-on experience through placement with major studios or on television movies and series, and education through mandatory seminars. The East Coast Program requires trainees to complete up to 350 days of on-set production work; the West Coast Program requires 400 days. While they are working, trainees are paid, beginning with a weekly salary of $487 in the East and $521 in the West. Once trainees have completed their program, they become freelance second assistant directors and can join the guild. The competition is extremely stiff for these positions; each location usually accepts 20 or fewer trainees from among some 800 to 1,200 applicants each year.

Keep in mind that Hollywood is not everything. Directors work on documentaries, on television productions, and with various types of video presentations, from music to business. Honing skills at these types of jobs is beneficial for those still intent on directing the big screen.

ADVANCEMENT

In the motion picture industry, advancement often comes with recognition. Directors who work on well-received movies are given awards as well as further job offers. Probably the most glamorized trophy is the Academy Award, also known as the Oscar. Oscars are awarded in 24 categories, including one for best achievement in directing, and are given annually at a gala to recognize the outstanding accomplishments of those in the field.

Candidates for Oscars are usually judged by their peers. Directors who have not worked on films popular enough to have made it in Hollywood should nevertheless seek recognition from reputable organizations. One such group is the National Endowment for the Arts, an independent agency of the U.S. government that supports and awards artists, including those who work in film. The endowment provides financial assistance in the form of fellowships and grants to those seen as contributing to the excellence of arts in the country.

EARNINGS

Directors' salaries vary greatly. Most Hollywood film directors are members of the Directors Guild of America, and salaries (as well as hours of work and other employment conditions) are usually negotiated by this union. Generally, contracts provide for minimum weekly salaries and follow a basic trend depending on the cost of the picture being produced: for film budgets over $1.5 million, the weekly salary is about $8,000; for budgets of

$500,000 to $1.5 million, it is $5,800 per week; and for budgets under $500,000, the weekly salary is $5,100. Motion picture art directors earn an average weekly salary of about $1,850, directors of photography about $2,000. Keep in mind that because directors are freelancers, they may have no income for many weeks out of the year.

Although contracts usually provide only for the minimum rate of pay, most directors earn more, and they often negotiate extra conditions. Woody Allen, for example, takes the minimum salary required by the union for directing a film but also receives at least 10 percent of the film's gross receipts.

Salaries for directors who work in television vary greatly based on type of project and employer, and on whether the director is employed as a freelancer or as a salaried employee. A director at a small-market station may average as little as $28,000 per year, while a director employed by a larger network affiliate may make up to $120,000 annually.

The U.S. Department of Labor reports that the median annual salary of film directors was $50,280 in 2000. Television directors earned approximately $34,630 a year. Among all directors, the lowest 10 percent earned less than $21,050, and the highest 10 percent earned more than $87,770.

WORK ENVIRONMENT

The work of the director is considered glamorous and prestigious, and of course directors have been known to become quite famous. But directors also work under great stress, meeting deadlines, staying within budgets, and resolving problems among staff. "Nine-to-five" definitely does not describe a day in the life of a director; 16-hour days (and more) are not uncommon. Because directors are ultimately responsible for so much, schedules often dictate that they become immersed in their work around the clock, from preproduction to final cut. Nonetheless, those able to make it in the industry find their work to be extremely enjoyable and satisfying.

OUTLOOK

According to the U.S. Department of Labor, employment for motion picture and television directors is expected to grow faster than the average for all occupations through 2010. This optimistic forecast is based on the increasing global demand for films and television programming made in the United States as well as continuing U.S. demand for home video and DVD rentals. However, competition is extreme and turnover is high. Most positions in the motion picture industry are held on a freelance basis. As is the case with most film industry workers, directors are usually hired to work on one film at a time. After a film is completed, new contacts must be made for further assignments.

Television offers directors a wider variety of employment opportunities such as directing sitcoms, made-for-television movies, newscasts, commercials, and even music videos. Cable television networks are proliferating, and directors are needed to help create original programming to fill this void. Half of all television directors work as freelancers. This number is predicted to rise as more cable networks and production companies attempt to cut costs by hiring directors on a project-to-project basis.

TO LEARN MORE ABOUT FILMMAKERS

BOOKS

Katz, Steven D. *Film Directing Shot by Shot: Visualizing from Concept to Screen.* Studio City, Calif.: Michael Wiese Productions, 1991.

Levy, Frederick. *Hollywood 101: The Film Industry.* Los Angeles: Renaissance Books, 2000.

Lindenmuth, Kevin J. *Making Movies on Your Own: Practical Talk from Independent Filmmakers.* Jefferson, N.C.: McFarland & Company, 1998.

Mamet, David. *On Directing Film.* New York: Penguin, 1992.

Weston, Judith. *Directing Actors: Creating Memorable Performances for Film and Television.* Studio City, Calif.: Michael Wiese Productions, 1999.

WEBSITES

American Film Institute (AFI)

www.afi.com

Visit this site for information on the AFI Conservatory, AFI workshops, AFI awards, and other film and television news.

Broadcast Education Association

www.beaweb.org

This is a good source of information on scholarships and grants, interest divisions, and filmmaking publications.

Directors Guild of America (DGA)

www.dga.org

Visit the DGA website to read selections from *DGA Magazine,* get industry news, and find links to film schools and film festivals.

www.dgatrainingprogram.org (East Coast program)
www.trainingplan.org (West Coast program)

These sites provide information on DGA's Assistant Directors Training Program.

Filmmaking.com

www.filmmaking.com

This site is a wealth of information on filmmaking. It includes interviews, links to filmmaking programs, online dictionaries for technical terms, and many other resources.

WHERE TO WRITE

American Film Institute (AFI)
2021 North Western Avenue
Los Angeles, CA 90027

Broadcast Education Association
1771 N Street, NW
Washington, DC 20036

Directors Guild of America (DGA)
7920 Sunset Boulevard
Los Angeles, CA 90046

HOW TO BECOME A PRODUCER

THE JOB

The primary role of a producer is to organize and secure the financial backing necessary to undertake a motion picture project. The director, by contrast, creates the film from the screenplay. Despite this general distinction, the producer often takes part in creative decisions, and occasionally one person is both the producer and director. On some small projects, such as a nature or historical documentary for a public television broadcast, the producer might also be the writer and cameraman.

The job of a producer generally begins in the preproduction stage of filmmaking with the selection of a movie idea from a script or other material. Some films are made from original screenplays, while others are adapted from books. If a book is selected, the producer must first purchase the rights from the author or his or her publishing company, and a writer must be hired to adapt the book into a screenplay format. Producers are usually inundated with scripts from writers and others who have ideas for a movie. Producers may have their own ideas for a motion picture and will hire a writer to write the screenplay. Occasionally a studio will approach a producer, typically a producer who has had many commercially or artistically successful films in the past, with a project.

After selecting a project, the producer will find a director, the technical staff, and the star actor or actors to participate in the film. Along with the script and screenwriter, these essential people are referred to as the package. Packaging is sometimes arranged with the help of talent agencies. It is the package that the producer tries to sell to an investor to obtain the necessary funds to finance the salaries and cost of the film.

There are three common sources for financing a film: major studios, production companies, and individual investors. A small number of producers have enough money to pay for their own projects. Major studios are the largest source of money, and they finance most of the big budget films. Although some studios have full-time producers on staff, they hire self-employed, or *independent producers*, for many projects. Large production companies often have the capital resources to fund projects that they feel will be commercially successful. On the smaller end of the scale, producers of documentary films commonly approach individual donors; foundations; art agencies of federal, state, and local governments; and even family members and churches. The National Endowment for the Humanities and the National Endowment for the Arts are major federal benefactors of cinema.

Raising money from individual investors can occupy much of the producer's time. Fund-raising may be done on the telephone, as well as in conferences, business lunches, and even at parties. The producer may also look for a distributor for the film even before the production begins.

Obtaining the necessary financing does not guarantee a film will be made. After raising the money, the producer takes the basic plan of the package and tries to work it into a developed project. The script may be rewritten several times, the full cast of actors is hired, salaries are negotiated, and logistical problems, such as the location of the filming, are worked out. On some projects it might be the director who handles these tasks, or the director may work with the producer. Most major film projects do not get beyond this complicated stage of development.

During the production phase, the producer tries to keep the project on schedule and the spending within the established budget. Other production tasks include the review of dailies, which are prints of the day's filming. As the head of the project, the producer is ultimately responsible for resolving all problems, including personal conflicts such as those between the director and an actor, and the director and the studio. If the film is successfully completed, the producer monitors its distribution and may participate in the publicity and advertising of the film.

To accomplish the many and varied tasks the position requires, producers hire a number of subordinates, such as associate producers, sometimes called coproducers, line producers, and production assistants. Job titles, however, vary from project to project. In general, *associate producers* work directly under the producer and oversee the major areas of the project, such as the budget. *Line producers* handle the day-to-day operations of the project. Production assistants may perform substantive tasks, such as reviewing scripts, but others are hired to run errands. Another title, *executive producer*, often refers to the person who puts up the money, such as a studio executive, but it is sometimes an honorary title with no functional relevance to the project.

REQUIREMENTS

There is no minimum educational requirement for becoming a producer. Many producers, however, are college graduates, and many also have a business degree or other previous business experience. They must not only be talented salespeople and administrators but also have a thorough understanding of films and motion picture technology. Such understanding, of course, only comes from experience.

High School

High school courses that will be of assistance to you in your work as a producer include speech, mathematics, business, psychology, and English.

Postsecondary Training

Formal study of film, television, communications, theater, writing, English literature, or art is helpful, as the producer must have the background to know whether an idea or script is worth pursuing. Many entry-level positions in the film industry are given to people who have studied liberal arts, cinema, or both.

In the United States there are more than a 1,000 colleges, universities, and trade schools that offer classes in film or television studies; more than 120 of these offer undergraduate programs, and more than 50 grant master's degrees. A small number of Ph.D. programs also exist.

Graduation from a film or television program does not guarantee employment in the industry. Some programs are quite expensive, costing more than $50,000 in tuition alone for three years of study. Others do not have the resources to allow all students to make their own films.

Programs in Los Angeles and New York City, the major centers of the entertainment industry, may provide the best opportunities for making contacts that can be of benefit when seeking employment.

Other Requirements

Producers come from a wide variety of backgrounds. Some start out as magazine editors, business school graduates, actors, or secretaries, messengers, and production assistants for a film studio. Many have never formally studied film.

Most producers, however, get their position through several years of experience in the industry, perseverance, and a keen sense for what projects will be artistically and commercially successful.

EXPLORING

There are many ways to gain experience in filmmaking. Some high schools have film and video clubs, for example, or courses on the use of motion picture equipment. Experience in high school or college theater can also be useful. One of the best ways to get experience is to volunteer for a student or low-budget film project; positions on such projects are often advertised in local trade publications. Community cable stations also hire volunteers and may even offer internships.

EMPLOYERS

Many producers in the field are self-employed. Others are salaried employees of film companies, television networks, and television stations. The greatest concentration of motion picture producers is in Hollywood and New York City. Hollywood alone has more than 2,000 producers.

STARTING OUT

Becoming a producer is similar to becoming president of a company. Unless a person is independently wealthy and can finance whichever projects he or she chooses, prior experience in the field is necessary. Because there are so few positions, even with experience it is extremely difficult to become a successful producer.

Most motion picture producers have attained their position only after years of moving up the industry ladder. Thus, it is important to concentrate on immediate goals, such as getting an entry-level position in a film company. Some enter the field by getting a job as a production assistant. An entry-level production assistant may Xerox copies of the scripts for actors to use, assist in setting up equipment, or perform other menial tasks, often for very little or even no pay. While a production assistant's work is often tedious and of little seeming reward, it nevertheless does expose one to the intricacies of filmmaking and, more important, creates an opportunity to make contacts with others in the industry.

Those interested in the field should approach film companies, television stations, or the television networks about employment opportunities as a production assistant. Small television stations often provide the best opportunity for those who are interested in television producing. Positions may also be listed in trade publications.

ADVANCEMENT

There is little room for advancement because producers are at the top of their profession. Advancement for producers is generally measured by the types of projects they do, increased earnings, and respect in the field. At television stations, a producer can advance to program director. Some producers become directors or make enough money to finance their own projects.

EARNINGS

Producers are generally paid a percentage of the project's profits or a fee negotiated between the producer and a studio. The U.S. Department of Labor (USDL) reports that producers and directors earned average salaries of $41,030 in 2000. Salaries ranged from less than $21,050 to more than $87,770. Producers of highly successful films can earn $200,000 or more, while those who make low-budget or documentary films might earn considerably less than the average. In general, producers in the film industry earn more than television producers. The USDL reports that producers employed in the motion picture industry had average earnings of $50,280 in 2000, while those employed in television broadcasting averaged $34,630. Entry-level production assistants can earn from less than minimum wage to $15,000 per year.

WORK ENVIRONMENT

Producers have greater control over their working conditions than most other people working in the motion picture industry. They may have the autonomy of choosing their own projects, setting their own hours, and delegating duties to others as necessary. The work often brings considerable personal satisfaction. But it is not without constraints. Producers must work within a stressful schedule complicated by competing work pressures and often daily crises. Each project brings a significant financial and professional risk. Long hours and weekend work are common. Most producers must provide for their own health insurance and other benefits.

OUTLOOK

Employment for producers is expected to grow faster than the average through 2010, according to the U.S. Department of Labor. Though opportunities may increase with the expansion of cable and satellite television, news programs, video rentals, and an increased overseas demand for American-made films, competition for jobs will be high. Live theater and entertainment will also provide job openings. Some positions will be available as current producers leave the workforce.

TO LEARN MORE ABOUT PRODUCERS

BOOKS

Erikson, Gunnar, Mark Halloran, and Harris Tulchin. *The Independent Film Producer's Survival Guide: A Business and Legal Sourcebook*. Omnibus Press, 2002.

Harmon, Renee. *The Beginning Filmmaker's Business Guide: Financial, Legal, Marketing, and Distribution Basics of Making Movies*. New York: Walker & Company, 1993.

Houghton, Buck. *What a Producer Does: The Art of Moviemaking (Not the Business)*. Los Angeles: Silman-James Press, 1991.

Levy, Frederick. *Hollywood 101: The Film Industry*. Los Angeles: Renaissance Books, 2000.

Rensin, David. *The Mailroom: Hollywood History from the Bottom Up*. New York: Random House, 2003.

WEBSITES

Producers Guild of America (PGA)

www.producersguild.org

Visit the PGA website to read an online version of *Point of View* magazine, which focuses on the role of producers in the motion picture and television industries.

Broadcast Education Association

www.beaweb.org

This is a good source of information on scholarships and grants, interest divisions, and filmmaking publications.

WHERE TO WRITE

Broadcast Education Association

1771 N Street, NW

Washington, DC 20036-2891

Producers Guild of America (PGA)

8530 Wilshire Boulevard, Suite 450

Beverly Hills, CA 90211

TO LEARN MORE ABOUT STEVEN SPIELBERG

BOOKS

Brode, Douglas. *The Films of Steven Spielberg* (revised ed.). New York: Citadel/Kensington, 2000.

Collins, Tom. *Steven Spielberg: Creator of E.T. (Taking Part Books)*. New York: Dillon, 1992.*

Conklin, Thomas. *Meet Steven Spielberg (A Bullseye Biography)*. New York: Random House, 1994.*

Connolly, Sean. *Steven Spielberg*. Des Plaines, Ill.: Heinemann, 1999.*

Ferber, Elizabeth. *Steven Spielberg*. Philadelphia: Chelsea House, 2000.*

Friedman, Lester D., and Brent Nothbohm. *Steven Spielberg Interviews*. Jackson, Miss.: University Press of Mississippi, 2000.

Gish, Melissa. *Steven Spielberg*. Mankato, Minn.: Creative Education, 2000.*

Gottfried, Ted. *Steven Spielberg: From Reels to Riches (Book Report Biographies)*. London: Franklin Watts, 2000.*

Horn, Geoffrey M. *Steven Spielberg (Trailblazers of the Modern World)*. New York: World Almanac Education, 2002.*

McBride, Joseph, *Steven Spielberg*. New York: Simon and Schuster, 1997.

Meachum, Virginia. *Steven Spielberg: Hollywood Filmmaker (People to Know)*. Springfield, N.J.: Enslow, 1996.*

Perry, George. *Steven Spielberg: Close Up*. New York: Thunder's Mouth Press, 1998.

Powers, Tom. *Steven Spielberg: Master Storyteller*. Minneapolis, Minn.: Lerner Publications, 1997.*

Rubin, Susan Goldman. *Steven Spielberg: Crazy for Movies*. New York: Abrams, 2001.*

Sanello, Frank. *Spielberg; The Man, the Movies, the Mythology*. Dallas, Tex.: Taylor, 1996.

Schoell, William. *Magic Man: The Life and Films of Steven Spielberg*. Greensboro, N.C.: Tudor, 1998.*

Silet, Charles, L.P. (ed.) *The Films of Steven Spielberg: Critical Essays*. Lanham, Md.: Scarecrow, 2002.

Sirimaroc, Elizabeth. *Steven Spielberg (Behind the Camera).* Philadelphia: Chelsea House, 2003.*

Taylor, Philip M., and Daniel O. Brien. *Steven Spielberg: The Man, His Movies, and Their Meaning* (3d ed.). New York: Continuum, 1991.

Woog, Adam. *Steven Spielberg (Inventors and Creators).* Detroit: Kidhaven/Gale, 2003.*

* Young Adult book

WEBSITES

Internet Movie Database
www.imdb.com

Spielbergfilms.com
www.spielbergfilms.com

Steven Spielberg Jewish Film Archive
sites.huji.ac.il/jfa/

Survivors of the Shoah Visual History Foundation
www.vhf.org

INDEX

Page numbers in *italics* indicate illustrations.

ABOUT THE AUTHOR

James Robert Parish, a former entertainment reporter, publicist, and book series editor, is the author of numerous biographies and reference books on the entertainment industry, including *Gus Van Sant, The Hollywood Book of Death, Jason Biggs, Whoopi Goldberg, Rosie O'Donnell's Story, The Unofficial "Murder, She Wrote" Casebook, Let's Talk—America's Favorite TV Talk Show Hosts, The Great Cop Pictures, Ghosts and Angels in Hollywood Films, Prison Pictures from Hollywood, Hollywood's Great Love Teams,* and *The RKO Gals*. Most recently he wrote the critically-lauded *The Encyclopedia of Ethnic Groups in Hollywood*. Mr. Parish is a frequent on-camera commentator on cable and network television for documentaries about the performing arts. Mr. Parish resides in Studio City, California.